A Straightforward Guide to

Writing Good Plain English
Improve Your Written English

Nicholas Corder

Straightforward Publishing
www.straightforwardpublishing.co.uk

Straightforward Guides

ISBN: 978-1-80236-104-9

Printed by 4edge www.4edge.co.uk
Typeset by Frabjous Books

Cover design by BW Studio Derby

Acknowledgements

This book is the result of running writing classes in a variety of different media, including scriptwriting, life writing, fiction and non-fiction in a wide variety of settings such as schools, colleges, libraries, universities, adult classes, prisons, and hospitals. I realised that many people were unsure of some of the basics of good writing. Not everyone has done higher studies in literature. Some people need a helping hand with grammar and punctuation.

Many of the available books on the subject range from the snide (can't you even punctuate?) to the dry and dusty. I've done my best to make sure the book is palatable, but you'll only ever get the tiniest proportion of the population to thrill to the thought of grammar and punctuation.

I must thank my students from whom this idea came. As ever, I'm indebted to my wife, Pauline, who reads early drafts and encourages me when the going gets tough. She also makes good coffee,

I'd also like to thank Roger at Straightforward Publishing who sticks with me as an author, despite the vagaries of the publishing world. This is the second edition of this book, so many thanks to him for giving me another crack at it.

Lastly, but most importantly, I'd like to thank you for either buying this book or borrowing it from the library. You are helping to keep the bailiffs from the door.

Also by Nicholas Corder

Non-Fiction

Escape from the Rat Race – Downshifting to a Richer Life
Learning to Teach Adults – An Introduction
Successful Non-fiction Writing
Foul Deeds and Suspicious Deaths in Staffordshire and the Potteries
Foul Deeds and Suspicious Deaths in Cumbria
Writing Your Own Life Story
Creating Convincing Characters

Fiction

The Bone Mill

Plays

Nigel's Wrist
Jacobson's Organ
Cash and Carrie
Star Struck
A Midsummer Night's Travesty
Shagathon
Bingo Royale
Fire in Her Belly
Talent
Catching Lightning in a Bottle
Twilight Robbery

Contents

Foreword   ix

1   Why Good Plain English?   1

2   The Steps of Writing   5

    Step 1 – Pre-writing – Ideas and Research   7

    Step 2 – Planning to Write   13

    Step 3 – Writing   20

    Step 4 – Re-writing – Editing and Redrafting   32

    Step 5 – Proofreading Your Work   40

    Step 6 – Presenting Your Work   46

3   A Potted History of English   49

4   How to Give Your Writing Zip   57

5   A Brief History of Grammar, Spelling
    and Punctuation   91

6   Some Hoary Old Grammatical Chestnuts   101

7   Confusable Words   118

8   A Quick Guide to English Grammar   147

9   Cutting out the Waste, Keeping the
    Writing Tight   160

10   A Quick Guide to Punctuation   165

11   Exercises – Over to You   189

12   Answers and Explanations   195

Appendix 1 – Useful Reading   207

Appendix 2 – How I Wrote This Book   209

Index   213

Foreword

Put it before them briefly so they will read it, clearly so they will appreciate it, picturesquely so they will remember it and, above all, accurately so they will be guided by its light.

Joseph Pulitzer.

Congratulations on picking up this book. You are a person of distinction and, if I may be so bold, you are easy on the eye. I like your hair. I like your clothes. I like the cut of your jib.

Now, before you take this book to the till, have the librarian swipe it onto your card, add it to your cyberspace shopping trolley, or even send it wirelessly to your e-book reader, let me tell you a little about the treats in store for you. That way, you know if it's worth shelling out your hard-earned cash and then spending several hours of your hectic life reading through what follows.

In a nutshell, this book aims to do exactly what it says on the cover — help you write good, plain English. The fact that you're reading this introduction means that you're the kind of person who would like to write well. You may be looking for a rule book. Beware of rule books. If there are such things as rules, they change quickly and are not always that helpful. This is a guidebook, not a straitjacket. You may even disagree with some of the things in here, and that's fine.

It is not a finger-wagging book. These are available. They have titles such as *If You Can't Even Write A Sentence You Must*

Be A Complete Prat, Only Total Divs Can't Spell or *Don't They Teach Them Anything at School Nowadays?* If you want to feel as though you've just crawled out of a sewer to be harangued by a man with a purple face, then please put this book down now and go and buy one of those. They are written by people who have never misspelled a word, cocked up a sentence or forgotten half-way through a paragraph what on earth it was they were writing about. This book is not meant to be a reprimand to some naughty child who's made a blooper. This book will not jeer at you if you get something wrong; it's meant to help you. It is a gentle book, a soft book. This book acknowledges that we're all human. It's the kind of book you could take home and introduce to your parents.

Writing is a genuinely difficult process. Don't let anyone tell you otherwise. Around one fifth of the population of the UK has genuine literacy problems and struggles with everyday written language. We're not helped by the fact that the English language is complex. It is a language that sucks in spellings and grammatical constructions from other languages. There are nine different ways of pronouncing the letter combination 'ough'. Challenge your friends to see if they can come up with them all. I will reveal more later.

The language changes constantly, adding new or newish words, such as *website, e-cigarette, permaculture.* There are words that are applied differently: *drone, woke, mouse.* We steal them from other languages: *samurai, ukulele, bungalow, croissant, Schadenfreude.* And then there are established words that go and change their meaning: *decimate, nubile, nice, terrible.*

Spelling is hard, as is grammar. Of course, this book tries to help you avoid the kind of grammatical howlers that have spittle-blowing retired colonels reaching for their fountain pens to condemn the current educational system. Yes, it's great to be able to spell correctly and stick the commas in the right place. So, we do have a bit of that in here. There are sections devoted to dealing with grammar, punctuation and confusable words. They're not the most interesting topics in the world, so you'll notice that all that stuff is towards the back of the book. The book is laid out using the principle that you shouldn't have to eat loads of soggy cornet wafer before you can get at the ice cream. Some sections, you'll only want to use for reference anyway.

But the book also tries to go a bit further than that. Sure, let's get the basics right, but let's also look at how to make what you write interesting — something that other people might want to read. What's the point of being able to spell and punctuate correctly if you can't convey your message to the reader?

And that's where our friend Pulitzer (the man quoted at the start) comes in. Good, plain English is what Pulitzer relished. Not just plain English, or good English, but a combination of the two. He was after more than just bare bones information. He wanted to be entertained, uplifted, carried along by the written word.

I don't expect you to read this book at a single sitting. Dip in and out of it as the mood takes you. Try to think about what you're reading and put it into practice when you can. Get some of those clever peel-off sticky labels and mark up the parts that are most relevant to you. Write in the margins, unless it's a library book. You can even do the exercises. Try not to cheat. Above all, don't turn reading this book into a chore, especially if it's been foisted on you by a teacher or lecturer or training manager.

And don't forget that this book contains mistakes of its own. I'd love you to think that these mistakes are deliberate, planted there to keep you on your toes. Alas, they're just mistakes.

But as I say. You're smart, good-looking, well-turned-out. We could have a future together. Click that button, swipe that card. Let's get going.

1

Why Good, Plain English?

Let's come back to something I touched on briefly in the foreword. Why both *good* and *plain*? Why not just *plain* English? After all, we know that clarity is important. We don't want to baffle the reader. Why not just keep it plain?

Plain English is excellent at reducing complex sentences to something more understandable. It cuts through the jargon and the gibberish. It removes redundant words and forces the writer to write in a straightforward manner. Of course, there is a place for it. You want it when you come across heart-sinking internal emails or signs on office walls, such as:

> *At the end of every working session, please ensure that the window latches in your office are secure as there has been a series of on-going thefts from offices recently and we are consequently worried about potential break-ins.*

It's long-winded. We are better off replacing it with something like:

> *Please lock your office windows when leaving the building — there has been a recent spate of thefts.*

That's plain English. You could make it even plainer, but let's not get too blunt. Plain English is also what we use in our everyday lives, so we don't have to dip into a pool of unfamiliar words. Using everyday language means we are more likely to create an immediate rapport with the reader, who is not going to be stumbling over awkward, unfamiliar terrain. If the reader immediately grasps what you are trying to say, then you have done the job well. The office windows should be locked.

If all we're doing is writing a few basic instructions, then short, plain language is fine. If we're trying to make sure that a member of the public buying our services understands potentially difficult terms and conditions clauses, then plain English is exactly what we need.

However, many of us often must write at a more complex level than this. We write essays and reports, press releases and conference papers. We need to be able to persuade, entertain or inform, without our readers dying of boredom.

The danger with plain writing alone is that it doesn't always reflect genuine complexities. It is also often dry and humourless. What we want is something that has a little bit of flair to it; something that has style, but which isn't stylised. We also want to engage the reader.

What is Good English?

Let's agree that plain English on its own is not enough for most types of writing. Where is the style? Where is that dynamic whiff of words well-chosen, sentences balanced, thoughts given wings? Where is the wit? We want something more than making a few word substitutions, using simpler vocabulary, or cutting down on sentence length.

'But,' I hear you cry. 'I work in the double-glazing industry and don't intend writing a novel. Why should I need my English to shine?'

To which I reply, 'so that your sentences are as clean and

shiny as your products.' (No, I didn't think it was funny, either.)

Good English is not the preserve of writers on the Booker shortlist. Here's an advertisement from a Marks & Spencer Catalogue:

> *Our luggage passes strict testing. Before we sell a piece of luggage, we:*
>> *Fill it with heavy items then drop it 8 times onto rough concrete*
>> *Squash, jerk and pull the trolley handle*
>> *And then, just for good measure, pull it over a bumpy road longer than the Great North Run.*

This is a deceptively clever piece of writing that is essentially aimed at selling suitcases. Admittedly, if you want to be pedantic and entirely literal you could argue that if you're about to buy the actual suitcase they've done all this to, that it might have already seen a lot of service and you'd like one that isn't scuffed and battered. But, if we sensibly accept that they've tested the model rather than the one you're buying, then it's great. Let's take a close look at it.

It would have been so easy to tell potential buyers that the luggage is tough and robust, with strong trolley handles. But it wouldn't have the same effect. Note the sparing, but clever use of adjectives (describing words). The items are *heavy*, the concrete is *rough* and the road is *bumpy*. Conditions are tough for this luggage. Then, we've got some great verbs (doing words) — *squash, jerk*. We've also got a throw-away phrase in *just for good measure* — as if it wasn't enough to do the first two things. And despite the fact that I suspect that 99% of the population has no idea how long the Great North Run is, it does sound like an enormous distance. In fact, it's a half-marathon — I looked it up. But *Great North Run* makes it sound as if that suitcase has

3

done more than a half-marathon. And it's tough up North. Just ask that Geordie in a T-shirt.

This is the kind of writing that typifies Good, Plain English. Writing it can be hard, because the actual process of writing is difficult. We'll break it down, though and now look at the steps that make up that process.

2

The Steps of Writing

Most of us have no notion of how professional writers go about their work. Why should we? Many people think that all the great novelists do is sit down and begin writing sentences that arrive wholesale from some mystical source. In their mind's eye, the great author is a kind of divining rod, channelling words that become phrases and sentences, paragraphs and books.

It would be fantastic if all flowed out exactly as we want it. But unless you're blessed with uncommon genius, it's not going to happen. For many writers, the actual production of the first draft itself is one of the shortest parts of the process. Actually, planning what to write and then refining what you have originally written may take far longer.

There are essentially six steps in the writing process:

- Pre-writing: the ideas and research stage
- Planning: getting those ideas into some kind of shape
- Writing: getting a first draft down on paper or computer
- Re-writing: editing and improving your work
- Proofreading: checking for mistakes
- Presentation: layout, diagrams, charts, tables, etc.

Frankly, with the exception of the last step, over which you may have no control, it's extremely difficult to separate these stages as they are interlocking components. Besides, different people will place more importance on one stage than on another. Some are fastidious planners; others tend to knuckle down quickly to writing. As the old cliché has it: there is more than one way to skin a rabbit. Indeed, accepting that we all work in a wide variety of ways is important. I can't reiterate strongly enough that finding your own way of approaching a writing project is vital. It's the product that counts, no-one really cares how you got there.

Similarly, not all of these steps require the same amount of time or work: some might need to be repeated. For instance, I do a great deal of rewriting as I like to get my first draft out as quickly as possible in the full knowledge that it will be extremely rough and require plenty of polish. Furthermore, obviously enough, the planning required for a hefty management report or a university dissertation is far greater than it would be for a shorter document.

Some steps overlap — when does jotting down vague ideas morph into actual planning or even writing? Does checking over what you wrote the day before count as re-writing? Or is it just a way of warming up to that day's efforts? When you discover you need to know more facts halfway through writing, does that count as pre-writing, planning, re-writing or what?

It's perhaps best not to think of writing as a linear process, but as a kind of spiral, where you keep on returning to what you've already done, pushing your work towards completion. In that case, let's accept that there's a little bit of falsehood in dividing the process into stages as we look at each step in turn.

For the sake of argument, I'm going to assume that the reader is about to embark on a longer project of factual writing, such as an essay or report. However, most of what I have to say applies to almost any piece of writing. Feel free to pick out the bits that are most relevant to you.

Step 1 Pre-writing – Ideas or research? Research or Ideas?

You may wonder why I have separated out the steps you take before starting your real writing into two distinct parts. I'll discuss the other pre-writing element, planning, more fully in a moment, but let's just say that planning is an organisational phase — it's about making decisions on the ordering of your work (and what to include or exclude). Right now, we're not even ready for that. We don't have any material to work on and need to get some together first. We need to be jotting down ideas, fragments, notes, quotations, research material — whatever you think might be the ingredients for your eventual piece of writing.

Again, as with so much to do with writing, it is often impossible to say with any certainty which comes first, ideas or research. One leads to the other and vice versa. For instance, whilst researching a compendium of local historical crimes, I was looking into the details of the hanging of a particular villain, when I came across another crime on the same page of the newspaper. It provided me with an additional chapter. The idea came from research. I was looking into something else completely.

It's up to you to develop an approach that suits you. Not feeling strait-jacketed by research might allow you to explore ideas more fully. On the other hand, researching what you're going to write may bring little nuggets that hadn't occurred to you. But we have to start somewhere, so let's assume you're starting with getting together basic ideas.

Brainstorming

One approach that is popular is brainstorming, which is a technique that is often used for problem solving. The concept behind it is that you note as many ideas as you can on a particular subject, without worrying whether those ideas are any good or not. At this stage, you don't want your gnomic internal critic saying, 'Well that's not very clever, is it?' before you've even got a single thing jotted down on a beer-mat. For now, you just want as many ideas as you can possibly come up with, from the mundane to the outrageous, from the essential to the ridiculous. You can work out later if your jottings are of any use.

You may have had to endure brainstorming as part of a group. One of the fallacies of the technique is that it is best performed by groups. In fact psychologists have proved that you're better off doing it alone, before joining other people and repeating the process. This creates the largest number of ideas. The difficulty, one suspects, is that if you're given the task of going away and thinking of new ways to make the sales floor more appealing to customers, you simply don't do it. Even with the best of wills, you get side-tracked into answering emails, dealing with staff and customers and so forth, so don't think about it at all until you're next in a formal meeting.

Once you've begun tossing around ideas, you'll then begin to see where you've got gaps. At this point, you might want to begin the more formal research phase, but don't forget that as you research a topic or a problem, what you discover can lead to more ideas. As I've already said, it's often impossible to separate the two.

Research

There's not the space here to deal with full-scale research, which means widely different things depending on what you're trying to do. However, let's assume that this may be the first time you've been asked to do a piece of extensive writing. Perhaps you're on a university course and suddenly have to put together a different kind of essay from what you wrote at school — an essay that needs thorough investigations, where you just can't check out a few facts on Wikipedia, but have to read books and journal articles and on-line sources to gather your material.

Or perhaps you've been asked to write an internal report. For instance, there have been a few problems with the bespoke software your company uses and you've been asked to look into specific difficulties and come up with suggestions for solutions. For this, you will have to do some form of enquiry to collect material — a questionnaire, interviews, case studies, observational studies. In other words, you need to be collecting data.

Even if you're asked to write an opinion piece (such as you find in newspapers on the editorial pages), you're still going to want to see what other people say, if only to try to avoid saying the same as them. No matter what your situation, you're going to have to do some kind of preliminary thinking and research.

Get a Notebook

To an extent, it doesn't matter how you organise your material at this point, it's collecting it that is important. We can worry about how we're going to use it at planning (or even, for you inveterate non-planners, writing) stage.

However, some kind of system for keeping all these ideas in one place is a must. If it's a large project, and you don't possess a hand-held gadget that will do the job for you, it might be worth dedicating a single notebook to it. Most writers I know are also stationery geeks. My stationery preferences are forever changing. However, I honestly think that the best size and shape of notebook is either the old-fashioned shorthand/reporters' notebook, which is wire-bound at the top, or a B5 notebook. If you can afford it, it's worth buying notebooks with slightly better quality paper as ink can easily be sucked through the pages of cheap paper. It's also quite useful if your notebook has a little built-in wallet at the back, although you can just as well glue an envelope in there. This is handy for scraps of paper. Think about having something pocket-sized for use on the go if you're not a mobile phone fan. You can copy up ideas into your master notebook at a later stage.

If you prefer hand-written notes, keep a fistful of pens of some sort about your person. Also handy are mechanical pencils with built-in erasers. Pencil writes on most surfaces and works better in the rain than ink. You also don't have to worry about keeping a mechanical pencil sharp and extra leads take up no room at all. Indeed, if you're working somewhere such as an archive, pens are probably banned anyway. It's also useful to have a box-file, basket or a wallet of some description at home. That way, if you've scribbled sudden ideas on a napkin or a bus ticket, you can keep those all in one place. It brings a touch of order to the chaos, without having to be the world's most efficient filing clerk.

Typing up your notes from time-to-time also means that your project is progressing. This is especially useful if you have to give precise bibliographic references. You can get the vital details of the book or journal, page number and so forth into the computer. When the time comes to prove that you didn't nick the idea, you have chapter and verse to hand and can simply cut and paste where needed. If you use a lot of direct quotations, it may be worth typing them up as you go along, which could save you a lot of time later. There's nothing more infuriating than needing to use a piece of information and not knowing where you got it from. Again, keeping a single computer file or folder for each project is good common sense.

Let It Marinate

All the time we're doing this preparatory work, we're going through a kind of process of marination, allowing our thoughts to range over what we might have to write.

In an ideal world, you'd have plenty of time between gathering all your notes, research and ideas together before sitting down to plan. In reality, we don't seem to allow ourselves any time to think. Somehow or other we have to be busy all the time. If our bosses find us with our feet up on the desk, wearing an eye-mask and ear-plugs, we're likely to face disciplinary action. Yet this would be a good way of actually coming up with ideas and seeing new solutions to problems.

Can you escape somewhere far from piped music and pneumatic drills, away from the drone of traffic and the general hubbub and busy-ness of the modern world? If you can, this gives your thoughts the opportunity to breath. Wordsworth famously described poetry as 'emotion recollected in tranquillity'. Of course, this is a romantic view, but still worth bearing in mind. A little bit of tranquillity helps us to think about what it is we're going to write. No wonder so many professional writers are inveterate dog-walkers. It gives them an excuse to be out of the house in the fresh air, away from computers and the desk, where they can actually let their minds breathe too.

Don't Push It

As you begin to gather facts, ideas and opinions, you're going to get to the stage where you're thinking, 'I've got a lot of stuff here. Do I really need any further information before I start the planning process?' If you've got obvious gaps, you might choose to plug them now, rather than leaving it till later. But if you get stuck, then there's no point in forcing the mind to work. Bizarrely, the human brain often works best when it is not actively engaged on what it should be doing. Einstein used to come up with his best ideas whilst he was noodling around on the violin. Leaving the subconscious to work on problems whilst getting on with something else is a good technique. Buy a violin. Or some noodles.

You'll possibly also come across material that you don't understand fully or that requires further investigation. This is especially true if you don't have much in the way of a mathematical background, then are suddenly expected to interpret charts, graphs or statistical tables. Statistics are a trap for the unwary. For instance, apparently UK divorce rates are lowest in the north-east of England. More men in the north-east have sheds than elsewhere in the country. The easy conclusion is that having a shed reduces your chance of divorcing. You'd love those two separate facts to be related, but they remain, alas, two separate facts — any link you make is purely conjecture.

You need to ask yourself if you really understand the data you have collected. Don't be afraid to ask for help. Revealing your ignorance at this stage will reflect better on you than revealing it in your final, fully written document.

To sum up, your pre-writing stage will include jotting, researching and marinating. You may have to call on other people to help. Above all, accept that this is just a preliminary process. Nothing is set in stone. You can always come back to this step. Don't worry if what you've got is a load of sticky notes in bad handwriting. This is where it all starts. But eventually we have to draw all this material together and begin our next step — planning.

Step 2 Planning to Write

Have you skipped the pre-planning step and come straight to this section? I suspect you're the kind of person who fancies skipping this step too and just firing up the computer and starting writing.

I know how you feel as I'm not the world's greatest planner either. Planning is hard work and if it doesn't come naturally to you, you can feel incompetent before you even start writing. You too might be the kind of person who just wants to get on with it, but a word or two of caution. Cracking on with it is fine if you have at least some general idea of what you're going to write. But if you sit down assuming that the blank page or screen will then suddenly provide you with the inspiration to write, you could be tempting fate.

Before we even start to think about what we're going to write, let's focus on the reader.

Who is Your Reader?

Imagine for a moment that you are thinking of setting up a Bed & Breakfast. Of course there are many factors you'll want to take into consideration, but one thing that you're going to want to do is to test out what it's like to be a guest. To do this, you might well spend a night or two in a letting bedroom, making sure the bed is comfortable, that the room isn't noisy and the en-suite shower works. In other words, you would put yourself in the position of the customer, the person on the receiving end of what you're trying to sell.

When it comes to writing, you need to try to do the same thing. You have to treat your reader with all the care and courtesy that you would expect to receive when you book into a B & B. Unless you are writing a diary or a journal that only you will ever read, then you need to bear in mind that at least one pair of eyes, other than your own, is going to read what you've written. You need a 'theoretical reader', but the difficulty is that we don't always know precisely for whom we are writing. Sure, an email addressed to one person has an obvious eventual reader. Similarly, a report written for people further up the chain of command has a limited and defined readership. But what happens if you're writing a sales brochure that almost anyone could pick up? Say, for instance, you sell garden sheds. Ordinary garden sheds, not the ultra-posh ones that double up as guest suites or luxury offices, but the kind we stick tools and old cardboard boxes in. Surely, almost anyone could buy one of those. Who is the reader of our brochure? We can't easily narrow down who we're writing for by age or social class. Yes, they're probably householders, but could be any age from 20-ish to 100, with any level of income or education, owners of a château or a tiny terraced house. The answer to the question, 'who is your reader?' is, 'well … er… almost anyone, really'.

What you then have to do is try to pick someone you know who might realistically read your brochure and aim your work at them. This sounds easy enough on paper, but is harder in practice. Of course, your theoretical reader is going to change according to circumstances. But bearing a real person in mind when you write is not a bad idea. Is your reader an expert, a novice, your boss, a professional, a teacher, a lecturer, a shopper at a certain store? Is it acceptable to use the jargon of your trade, or is the reader likely to stop reading if you use technical vocabulary?

To sum up, there are some basic questions you need to ask yourself:

- Who is your reader?
- What is your reader's level of skills and knowledge?
- What is your reader's educational level?
- How much jargon will they already know?
- How should I then pitch my writing?
- How am I going to come across to the reader?

Now, let's start thinking about the content of what we're writing. Before you start trying to organise your notes into any semblance of order, it's worth asking yourself this fundamental question: what is your basic idea?

For most of us, the basic idea of what we're going to write is imposed from outside. Someone sets us a task. This might be to write an essay, a report, a letter, a proposal or some web pages. Form and content are interwoven. Web pages are often picture-led, whereas a report might need to contain analyses of statistics and closely written text. We have to dance to someone else's tune.

Strangely, it's often easier when someone tells you what to write. You may not like what you've got to do, but at least you know what is wanted. When given a free choice of subject, my students often have great difficulty on settling on a topic or an idea. They find that being given a specific task to do (or a limited range of choices) is far easier. You're not starting from absolute zero, as you might be if you were going to write a speculative article for a magazine. Asking someone to write specifically about a subject automatically gives focus to the task.

If, on the other hand, you are going to have to write something entirely from scratch, then you're going to need to work out what it is you're trying to say. At this point, it's worth looking at your notes and deciding what is central. Try to distil what you're trying to do into a brief summary. Exactly what are you trying to say? Can you summarise your idea in one sentence? How would you tell someone what you're doing in 20–25 words?

If you're writing a novel, then how would the little listing in the *Radio Times* describe the film of your book? If you're writing an essay — leaving aside more cynical thoughts that you're doing it because if you don't, you get no marks — what is your fundamental idea? If your fundamental idea then doesn't match with the title or question of the essay, then maybe you need to re-direct what you're doing. Does the brochure you're putting together to sell a product actually sell that product?

Yes, there is a danger that something you want to say might become simplistic, but more often than not, the precise focus of this exercise forces you to recognise what is important in your notes or what is surplus to your needs and can be ditched.

If you want to concentrate even harder on the fundamental purpose of your writing, copy your sentence onto a piece of card and stick it to the frame of your laptop or tape it to your desk. Then it's a constant reminder, bringing you back to the central point of your writing — to its heart.

How Much Planning Before You Start Writing?

Again, only you can answer this question. As I've already confessed, to this day, I still have a tendency to bash stuff out with half a plan in mind, then organise it properly later. So don't regard what follows as a rigid approach, but do bear in mind that if you skip some of the early steps, or fudge them, or gloss over them, you will still eventually have to impose order on chaos. In other words, you will have to plan, even if you do so after you've written a first draft.

On the other hand, you may be an exacting planner full of clever foresight. My schoolteachers would have loved you. Educating for accuracy and logic, rather than creativity, they expected everything to be in place before any of their charges had uncapped their fountain pens. That's the other extreme. If you can do that, fine. But for most of us, it's unrealistic. Few of us are able to be as logical as this. And if we are, we're probably writing computer code rather than reports and essays. Besides, even if we think we have planned everything down to what we feel might be the last detail, then putting something into practice always involves changes. The majority of you will land somewhere in the middle. You need to do some kind of formalised planning, especially if you're dividing the work amongst colleagues, but it doesn't all have to be entirely in place before you start writing.

For the moment, let's look at those rough jottings, quotations, questionnaires and random ideas you've collected so far. We now need to think about some way of re-arranging our notes into something that has shape to it. In other words how are you going to organise your thoughts? For some people, this seems to come entirely naturally. For most of us, this is one of the hardest parts of writing. Let's look at two contrasting methods.

Mindmapping versus Linear Notes

There are essentially two main types of plan — diagrammatic or linear.

A common type of diagrammatic plan is the mindmap. This is a term coined by Tony Buzan, although he was not the first to come up with the idea of using diagrams to organise notes. The essential idea is that you place your key word in the centre of your page, then create a kind of tree and as information occurs to you, you add it to branches or twigs, depending on how important each element is. You may also have come across terms such as cognitive map, fish-boning, concept map, spidergram or tree diagram. These are all variations of mindmaps, and whilst there are differences between them, for now, let's just stay with the idea that the mindmap is a diagram of ideas.

Type the word *mindmapping* into an Internet search engine and you'll be inundated with a veritable Garden of Eden of beautiful, multi-coloured trees, with curling branches and twigs all neatly labelled. You can make such a diagram as pretty, and as complex, as you want. Advocates love a mindmap; they say that its advantage over other forms of planning is that it gives them an overall picture of a topic that they can take in at a single glance. If they then think of another idea, they can easily add it in a relevant place. They feel that this kind of diagram gives them a fuller picture. Anything that helps you organise thoughts is great, so if mindmapping appeals to you, then it's worth trying it out.

On the other hand, maybe you've already tried mindmapping and don't like it. Or perhaps it's something you've not used before and suspect that by the time you've learnt how to use it effectively, you could have written your document with time to spare for an evening down the pub. Then there's no reason why you should use it. Writing is hard enough without using a technique that doesn't work for you.

Besides, writing is actually a linear process. We work our way through the text line by line. Even if you have the world's most beautiful mindmap, so perfect it could be handed down the generations to keep the flame of your genius alive, at some point it needs to become a piece of writing, and thus linear. Of course, the same also holds true for those of you who only have three scratty post-its and a cigarette packet covered in barely-legible hieroglyphs.

If you jot your notes down the page in straight(-ish) lines, then it's also worth thinking about using bullet points rather than numbers. If you start by numbering your ideas, that tends to give them different levels of importance. Idea 1 must be more important than idea 2. Idea 2 is more important than idea 3 and so on. With bullet-points, you know that it's not a hierarchy, but simply ideas on paper that just happen to be in a line on a page. Order can come later.

One way of moving on towards a linear plan might be to write each major point on a card. Spread them over your desk or table and see what you've got. Does anything stand out as an obvious topic heading? If so, move these to the top of the table, then simply move round your other cards until you think you've got them into some kind of order. You can then simply gather them up and type them up into a word-processor in the order you've decided on. You should now be able to answer two vital questions: What individual bits of information do you want to get across? What order do these need to be in?

The structure of what you're going to write may be predetermined by your employer or institution. If it isn't, you may need to do some research into what format is required. There are several books available on business writing that deal with specific formats that are useful for the workplace. Having a format to your work is a help, not a hindrance. But you may have to create your own format. Most of it is common sense. For instance, a research-based management report often contains the following components:

- Title
- Purpose of the report
- Research methods
- Examination of findings
- Conclusions
- Recommendations
- Executive summary (one page précis)

Whatever the format, it's good to arrive at the writing stage with a paragraph-by-paragraph breakdown of what you're going to write. It's also good if you can see what line any argument you have to make is going to take. Then, when you've got some idea of how your plan is shaping up, you can ask yourself:

- What's missing? Have you left out something obvious?
- Do you need to marinate the idea more?

But what happens if you get stuck?

If you can't manage to organise yourself at this stage, don't panic. Try deciding on what goes where again, without worrying too much that everything is in place. Look for alternative ways to think through your organisation. Perhaps this time, you could use a spreadsheet, stick a topic on each line, then cut and paste them where they need to go. Maybe colour-coding your ideas will work, it certainly makes them prettier and therefore more fun to look at.

But if you still have no joy and are really in a jam, then maybe just starting to write is a good idea. Pick one element of your project and start writing that. It doesn't matter which part. Modern computer apps mean that you can sew it all together later. I've already described the writing process as a spiral. You may find that writing something actually helps you bring ideas into focus — you can loop back to planning later.

Step 3 Writing

You can plan as much as you like, but at some point you're going to have to get started! This is when we get to:

The First Draft

The biggest block to writing is thinking that you have to get it right first time. You don't. Nobody has to see the real mess you make early in the process. In her book *Becoming a Writer*, first published in 1934, but still in print, Dorothea Brande writes about the brain having two contradictory halves. One is the free-flowing, idea-manufacturing, often whimsical side that brings in all your creativity. The other side is that critical side that provides rational thought. It's the free-flowing side of your brain that you want now, just as it was when you were first coming up with ideas for what to write. You can be as messy as you like.

I often compare my method of working to the scene in *Close Encounters of the Third Kind*, where Richard Dreyfuss is sent telepathic signals about where the aliens are going to land. He heaps huge dollops of mashed potato onto a plate and then begins sculpting it into the shape of the mountain. For your first draft, all you have to do is slap dollops of mashed spud into a dish. You don't need to worry if any drops on the floor, or if there are chunky bits in it that shouldn't be there, or if the top is too high or the peak too sharp. All you're doing is creating the basic raw material from which you are to sculpt the finished mountain. That's my way. But here are some tips to help you discover your way.

Try not to be Writerly

We've all come across the kind of moronic gobbledygook that should carry a health warning. The people who write psychobabble seem to be more concerned with how important they sound than with what they're saying. They are focused on themselves and not the reader. It's an easy trap to fall into.

Writing is an introspective business and, more often than not, a solo task.

We have the added difficulty that when we sit down to write, we are slipping from one mode of communicating to another. If we have an important speech or business presentation to make then we don't talk as if we're chatting down the pub. Likewise, the moment we start thinking about producing our words in a formal written form, rather than a matey email or text, for instance, we seem to change our thought processes.

That's good in one way. Written language needs much more formal organisation than spoken language. If you've ever read a transcript of a conversation, you'll see that most people speak in half-finished sentences, with plenty of speech tics (ums and errs). It is almost impossible to follow. Written language requires us to write in proper sentences and to throw in punctuation marks to guide the reader. But I suspect that when we sit down to write, we go a step further than that. Maybe, when we roll up our sleeves, uncap the pen and fire up the computer, a little voice inside says, 'You are writing now, so you need to be writerly'.

Suddenly, what we produce has an extra layer of pomposity. We turn in on ourselves, sweating over the labour of getting it all out of our heads and onto the screen. We lose sight of the fact that someone — and a real person at that — is going to read this. We start writing in a way that doesn't sound anything like us. We assemble the poshest vocabulary and spew it mercilessly onto the page. We don't write about dogs, we have canine friends. We don't have a tooth pulled, we have dental extractions. We don't move fast, but with alacrity.

Try to forget that you are writing. Try simply to let the words flow as they would if you were addressing a meeting or explaining something aloud to a colleague or friend. It is much easier to tighten up what you've written at a later stage to make it sound less chatty than it is to loosen up pomposity.

How Long Can I Put off Writing?

One of my relatives dropped round a while back to see if I could give her a hand. She was preparing a mini-dissertation of 10,000 words based on a research project as part of a professional qualification. To give you some idea of how much work this is, if you were to print the finished dissertation, using generous margins, headers and footers, double-spacing and a normal 12-point font, you would use around 35-40 sides of A4. This is also typically the minimum length of an undergraduate dissertation.

Ostensibly she wanted to discuss the contents of her project. However, what became obvious was that she knew exactly what she wanted to write, but had simply stalled. The actual writing-up of the project had become bigger and bigger in her mind. It was now disproportionately huge and daunting, so she dreaded doing it.

She's not the only person who feels that way. When I supervised undergraduate dissertations or extended essays, my students were often bursting with ideas. They might even have pages of notes and fancy-pants mindmaps with beautiful colour coding. But the thought of producing 10,000-12,000 words seemed overwhelming. Where do they start? How much planning should they do before starting to write? Several would end up over-researching, not because they needed to know more, but because doing research meant they were 'working' on their projects, but postponing the dreaded moment when they had to take everything they'd been thinking about and convert it into a piece of writing.

You no longer have the excuse that you don't know what to

write. You are now on an entirely new excuse — that the actual task of writing all this is intimidating. Don't fancy painting your hallway? Fine. Call in a decorator. Don't want to weed the borders? Get a gardener. Don't want to write the piece of work that only you can write? Tough. Only you can do it.

There are so many delaying tactics for writing, that one day I might write a whole book on them. The book you hold in your hand was subject to many delays, few of which were caused by genuine problems, but by the fact that writing something this length is a big project. It simply takes longer to write than, for instance, a magazine article, so there are many things you can find to do instead of getting on with it.

You have to accept that you're not going to get it finished at a single sitting unless you have unlimited access to amphetamines (not a recommended path). Natural interruptions are added to by delaying tactics of your own invention. Did I really need to sharpen my entire biscuit-tin full of pencils before I could start work? How neat should a desk drawer be?

I'm not alone. Almost every professional writer I know will find ways to procrastinate. If people who get paid to produce words for a living find it hard to knuckle down, what about people for whom it's just a small part of the job, or who don't get a penny for their efforts?

There's an essay due in at the end of the month. Four weeks in which to write it. So you start the night before the deadline. (And, yes, I did this when I was a student, so I know how you feel.) You have a report to put together and the more you put off knuckling down to it, the bigger it gets, until the deadline looms up like the iceberg in front of the Titanic, bringing with it paralysed fear. Leave a writing project too long and the job looks harder and harder.

Deadlines Are Good for You

I once pitched an idea to a magazine editor. It was for what they call a *timeless piece*. In other words, it didn't have to be in a particular issue to fit with dates or seasons. He bought the idea, but wasn't in a hurry for it. I'm certain that if he'd asked for them by lunchtime, I'd have got them to him by then. The 1,500 words might have been slightly less polished, but he'd have had them. Instead, it became the constant back-burner job. Eventually, he got the article 13 months after he'd accepted it.

A deadline is good. Yes, sometimes people want our work too quickly, so we end up with a rushed job that could have been a lot better. But, in the main a cut-off date helps. If you can, negotiate yours. Give yourself enough time to do the job well, but not so much time that the project actually slips from your grasp. The more you understand yourself as a writer, then the better you will become at knowing how much time you realistically need.

Bite-sized Chunks

Imposing your own deadlines is especially useful if you have an enormous project. A book, obviously, takes a long time to write. Normally, you will agree a deadline with a publisher. Typically, for a book such as this one, this might be around nine months to a year ahead.

Now, to begin with, that looks easy enough. It looks like plenty of time, but a big project generally needs sub-dividing. Just clattering away to a cut-off date perhaps a year away is probably no use. Too many words. Too much time. If a book is 12 chapters, you could organise yourself to do one a month, but what happens if a chapter stalls, or in the writing of it, you discover that the material should really be elsewhere in the book? Or it proves irrelevant and you're a chapter short? Or you fall ill?

If you can divide your project into sections, that's great. It might also give you an idea of how many words you need for each part. I set myself word targets, rather than chapter targets. That way, if I feel stuck on a particular part of a book, I can skip to somewhere else, not feel bogged down and go back to it later. My software also has a daily target that I have set for 1,000 words. I sometimes even get graph paper and colour in the squares to represent how many words I've written. It's a kind of visual bribe.

Many writers will be a good deal faster than I am; others slower, more painstaking. Some days you'll decide you don't like a couple of pages you've written and cut them. Your daily target just got harder. Some days, your fingers will fly. I have a rule that if I need to produce 1,000 words today and I produce 2,000, that doesn't give me the day off tomorrow, it just puts me ahead of schedule and gives me more time for revisions. If I'm running writing workshops, then there may not be time to write anything of my own at all other than handouts, sometimes for several weeks.

Most importantly, this is what works for me. I don't suggest that this is exactly what will work for you. Be wary of writers who tell you it must be done their way, and no other. Bearing in mind that caveat, I still think that the easiest way round the problem of delaying writing is to divide it into chunks. It's always easier to maintain momentum than it is to get going in the first place. Essentially, if you're writing anything substantial, you're not going to finish it in one day. You will also run out of steam at some point and what you produce will become sub-standard. You can't do tomorrow's writing today; you can only write what you can write. Set yourself interim deadlines and do your utmost to stick to them.

If you find even this too daunting, then just sit down and write for 10 minutes. At least you'll produce something, even if it's just 50 or 100 words. You may find that an hour has gone and you've knocked off a couple of pages of first draft. You may find it useful to have a look at a time management idea called the Pomodoro Technique, where you divide work into 25 minute chunks.

Don't Worry about Introductions and Conclusions

Fretting about exactly how to start a piece of work can often lead to frustration. You can spend ages trying to work out how to start. If you've already thought of a neat way of introducing your work then that's fine. If not, don't get in a muck sweat about it. You may find that writing your document out in full makes you realise exactly how you should start it. Besides, modern computer apps are brilliant. If your starting paragraph or introductory section occurs to you as you're writing one thing, you can always interrupt what you're doing, write the opening and then come back to where you were.

Don't Worry about Your First Draft

Yes, the thought of producing a big document for your line manager or your first major university essay may be daunting, but there's only one way to get over that. Start writing. Don't worry if it is any good or not. Just start writing. The computer is your friend. We've seen that it allows you to cut and paste work together. It permits you to work in a fashion that isn't necessarily logical. Just get something, anything at all, written. Shape, form, spelling, grammar, accuracy, polish and so forth can all come later.

Nobody should get to see your first draft. But remember, if you don't have a first draft, you won't have anything at all.

Do Not Compare Yourself to Others

Those who do have genuine literary flair are placed on pedestals in the Pantheon. The rest of us look up in awe of them, frightened that what we might produce is shoddy in comparison. The literary greats burst with ideas, crafted into well-honed sentences.

If you think for one moment that you're competing with them, you won't write a word. Don't compare yourself to Dickens or Austen or Balzac or whoever you think is a literary giant. If you do, you will sit there sucking your pencil, or surfing the Internet looking for funny cat videos instead of writing.

Find Your Best Method

If you read books on writing (and you are reading one right now), you may find the author giving you precise directions on how to go about writing. As I've already said and will probably say again: be wary of this. You need to find a way of writing that suits your temperament, the time you have available and your working habits. Inveterate planners will fill a notebook before they begin writing in earnest. Others will start writing and see where they get. The important thing is to find out how you work. If the method you settle on seems like an odd way of working, don't chastise yourself; just accept that it's your way of doing things, but get on with it.

Find the Best Place to Write

If you can write anywhere, that's great. If you can't, you may find that you need somewhere quiet, or somewhere that is just devoted to writing. I'm lucky; I have a converted summerhouse where I do all my writing. It's crammed full with books and reference materials and stationery and everything else that I need. It has a door that I can shut and only room for one person.

Most people find it hard to write in noisy open-plan offices. If you have a long document to write, it may be worth asking your boss if you can work from home or book out a meeting-room to get a first draft done.

Avoid Distractions

Even if you're working at home, there are plenty of other things you can do to help you avoid doing any actual writing. Computer games and the Internet are excellent for this — they look vaguely like work as they take place on-screen and you normally sit at a desk to do them.

If you can find a way of minimising distractions, then it's not a bad idea. The author Will Self found that working on a computer was providing too many web-based distractions, so he went back to using a typewriter for his early drafts. There's also something to be said for writing in longhand. A writer friend of mine swears by his fountain pen. He likes the feel of ink over paper and it forces him to think through what he's writing before committing a sentence to paper. I have used a device called an Alphasmart, a basic word-processor, and a Pomera, similar, but smaller. I also like good quality Japanese pencils onto which I put rubber grips and write long-hand.

Years ago, the telephone was the constant interrupter. I partially solved it by buying an ansaphone and phoning back when it suited me, but still ended up hovering over the machine as the messages came in, just in case it was anything important. Nowadays that telephone is in your pocket all the time and texts, the web and email are the killers. The web is probably worst. The instant accessibility of vast, roiling vats of cyber-info is such a temptation. Whereas a decade or two ago you'd have to check a spelling in a paper dictionary or the capital of Lesotho in your encyclopaedia, nowadays, you just click on the mouse and away you go. The trouble is that you don't just end up knowing the capital of Lesotho (Maseru), but discover that it is an enclave, as is Vatican City. Vatican City has a population of only ... and so on, until eventually you're on a website describing the virtues of the Garibaldi biscuit and an hour has passed.

If you're disciplined, you can keep from researching the little bits and pieces you need instantly. I use the system of inserting 'xxxx' to mark a place in the text I need to come back to. I then just press 'find' and look for 'xxxx'. Alternatively, you could just keep a paper list.

Email is hard. When I first started using it, in the days of dial-up, I thought it was the bee's knees. It saved the price of a stamp and was a kind of *poste restante.* You weren't interrupting the person you emailed and they could reply when it suited them. Some people are extraordinarily disciplined and only open emails twice a day, but the difficulty is that all the technology has become portable. Email can be picked up on a mobile phone and the person sending it now often expects an immediate reply.

Pen and Paper or Computer?

Use whatever method suits you. Most writers I know tend to go straight to the computer, but have already got some jottings in a notebook. Others like to write their first draft by hand. The obvious advantage of handwriting is that you can write anywhere under almost any conditions. All you need is a notebook and a few sharpened pencils. It also means that when you type up your work, you can turn it into a second draft by making changes as you go.

One piece of advice that I think is worth sharing is that it's a good idea not to develop too many rituals around your writing. If you can only write if you have your favourite gonk on the end of a Staedtler black and red striped HB pencil in a Moleskine notebook, with your desk facing the East and the toilet seat firmly shut to avoid bad Feng Shui, then you're going to have trouble.

I Think I've Got Writer's Block

Having writer's block does seem a bit fanciful. To be honest, it's best left to arty-farty types talking loudly in couscous restaurants. But I'm sure that most of us have had that awful sensation of staring at blank screen or a white page. Nothing comes. Nothing. The screen becomes blanker and the page whiter.

I'm not sure I've got the solution to this, but suspect that if you're sitting there, unable to produce anything, then you shouldn't be sitting there at all. Leave your work space and go and make yourself a cup of coffee, walk the dog. Try to find yourself a breather away from the hustle and bustle of the office or the kids or your slacker flat-mates.

If you find that you spend ages staring at a blank sheet of paper and that all that then happens is that you become frustrated or convinced that you're incompetent and you'll be out of a job by the end of the week, then maybe you need to think slightly more about preparation.

Above all, think of the process of writing as simply another task to be done rather than some vast, over-facing chore. If you can regard it as being just one more thing on your daily round of answering the phone, dropping the kids off at school, making sandwiches or whatever, then it will cease to grow in importance in your mind.

There's no denying that it helps to be in the mood to write. But if professional writers waited for perfect conditions, then they'd not make a living. You'll often hear novelists saying things such as, 'I'm inspired every morning at nine o'clock.' Nevertheless, there are times when it is harder to write than others. For instance, I find when I've finished a large project, such as a book, I have a lot of difficulty getting going on something else. If only I were more like the novelist Anthony Trollope, who used to write for two hours before going out to work and when he finished one novel, he just ruled off the page and started on the next. But we can't all be Anthony Trollope, so I live with this hand-wringing and try to fill my time usefully with admin tasks that have been postponed whilst I've had my head down.

Step 4 Rewriting — Editing and Redrafting

Your first draft, indeed anyone's first draft, is never good enough. Let's reiterate that people who don't understand the process of writing often think that professional writers simply spill out words and the job's a good'un. But no professional writer would think for a moment that their first effort would pass muster. You should adopt the same approach. The reality is that almost everything you see in print will have been through several versions, then often handed onto someone else who can cast a neutral eye over the work and suggest improvements. If at any point you are 100% pleased with what you've written, then that's a sure sign that you haven't done enough work.

In this section, we're going to look at how to re-write. I'm going to use the terms editing, re-writing, and re-drafting more-or-less interchangeably, although there are some subtle distinctions. Most importantly, we're still talking about the process of writing. We're not talking about proofreading, which is simply the picking up of typos or occasional bits of soggy grammar. In fact, one of the hardest parts of re-drafting is stopping yourself from jumping to the proofreading step straight away. The temptation is to start putting in the missing commas and straightening the wayward bits of syntax. But when you re-draft, you need to be looking at the bigger picture. Nor is editing a one-off activity, unless you're under an unrealistic deadline.

For me, the editing process is probably the most important step in writing. It's also extremely hard. You've just trained yourself to bash out words without worrying too much about what you're writing, then suddenly you have to flick a switch and become your own critic. Re-writing is also at its most difficult when you have little time between your first and second drafts. You're too familiar with the content. It is extraordinarily difficult suddenly to become dispassionate about your work and see it as though you were reading it for the first time.

Have you ever seen those TV programmes where people are failing to sell their house because they've got a bit too much clutter and the hall's a bizarre purple colour? Often potential buyers can't see beyond this. Well, your first draft can have as much clutter as it likes and the hall can be purple, vermilion, zebra-striped or the colour of school custard. At the moment, you don't have potential purchasers. You know you're going to have to de-clutter and re-decorate.

This first draft is for your eyes only. As a rule, I am extremely reluctant to show anyone a first draft of anything I've written. Indeed, the only time I would allow any students or course participants to do so is if we're trying out stuff in the seminar or training room, when we've all just jotted something down and are thus all in the same boat. None of the elements that go into good writing matters at this point. Your spelling can look like an accident with a Scrabble set. Your grammar can make you sound semi-literate. Your punctuation can be as wobbly as a sailor on shore leave. You don't even necessarily have to have anything resembling structure yet. None of this matters. You have a first draft and can now do what you like with it.

However, once you've been through a second draft yourself, if you can involve someone else in your work, now is the time to do it. Fresh eyes will spot things that you've missed. But give your editorial reader a clear brief, one based on the grounds we're about to cover. This is crucial, because there are two main editorial stages:

First, there is editing for content, where we look at what we've got missing, what we've repeated, where our ideas aren't clear or the ordering of information isn't as clever as it might be.

Second, once we have the content we're looking for, we can re-write to clarify meaning, add a bit of style and panache and generally pimp our prose.

If you hand over a draft to anyone else for advice, you must brief them fully. Are you after help with the content and logic of your piece, or do you want to tighten up the actual style? At this step, it's pointless passing on a piece of work where you know there are problems with content, to find that your reader has simply stuck in a few commas and circled a typo or two.

Before you start on the editing process, print out your work, double-spaced, leaving nice chunky margins. That way, there's plenty of space for new material. Viewing your work on paper looks totally different to viewing it on screen and somehow makes it almost like a new work. Don't be frightened to make wholesale changes if necessary.

When you come to do amendments on the computer, it's not a bad idea to copy and paste all your work across into a new file, which you can then mark as version 2, 3, 4 or whatever. That way, if you suddenly find that you've over-edited something, or you preferred an earlier version, you can always go back to it.

Editing for Content

There's no point editing your work for style if you haven't got the content right. So before you start weaning out the clichés and the passives (see *verbs* in the grammar section for an explanation of this), you need to concentrate on these four main points:

- Adding missed information, including your introduction, conclusion and executive summary (if needed)
- Altering and developing ideas
- Restructuring – moving paragraphs and sentences, deleting sections that are irrelevant or don't work
- Correcting factual errors

If you started your draft from a well-developed plan, then you can check against it to make sure you've covered all the points you wanted to include. Simply get a copy of that plan — linear or mind map or whatever — and as you read back through what you've written, cross off the points you've made as you get to them. If you've crossed everything off your plan, it doesn't necessarily mean that your work is complete, but at least it means that you've covered everything you'd thought of originally.

Now, if you're a non-planner or a semi-planner, you probably don't have some neat diagram to compare your draft to. In this case, what you can now do is write your plan. Yes, really. As you read through each paragraph, just note down what each one is telling you. You will end up with a list of what you've got in your draft. Importantly, it also means that you have this information in a different format, which is often a good way of looking at your work with fresh eyes.

Whichever way you go about it, if you find that you've got a paragraph that essentially doesn't tell us anything, is there a reason to keep it in? Again, if in doubt, take each paragraph in turn and write alongside it the key point you are making. We want the padding to come out, after all.

Order, Order

In many ways, that's the easy bit. A much harder question is, 'have I got everything in the right order?'

To some extent, you can't win with this. Whatever you choose is not necessarily going to fit with everyone else's logic. As a personal example, I've hummed and hawed over whether the section of this book devoted to the steps of writing (i.e. the section we're in now) should come before or after the tips on what makes good writing. I'm still not sure. If I give the writing tips first, people will know about style and so forth before they put pen to paper. Read about the steps of writing and you'll understand more about the process, but may not be as confident about style. There is no correct way; I just had to make a guess, based on instincts and experience. Besides, there is no rule to say you have to read this book in the order I've given you. I always read conclusions first.

One method that I sometimes use is to physically cut and paste up an early draft. Yes, this can be done on the computer, but printing out the draft, then taking scissors to it and moving the various sections around the dining table works better than doing it on the computer. Perhaps it's another case of a new format helping you to visualise your work slightly differently. A roll of sticky tape or a glue stick and some rough paper are handy. Then, once you've got a physical order to your work, you can go back to the computer and use its inbuilt cut & paste facility. Yes, it does often mean that you have to re-write some of the linkages at the start and end of paragraphs, but it also helps show where your work may have come slightly adrift. Indeed, writing these new links may make you think exactly how you are going to signpost your reader from one point to the next.

Writing Introductions and Conclusions

When you've got all this stuff organised, then you can also think about your introduction and your conclusion (assuming you need them). You'll now have a good idea of what the essence of your document is. Well-written introductions and conclusions are vital. They must not at any time feel like a bolt on added extra, simply there to make the word count or bulk out the report.

A good introduction lays the ground for what is to come. It doesn't leap into the action, but tells us what to expect. However, essays are particularly prone to overlong introductions that are vague, waffly and indirect. Certainly, when marking essays, I would often find that a student could lose most of the first page. In a 3,000-word essay, wasting one tenth of its length on irrelevant material that lacks focus is a missed opportunity to shine. I suspect that overlong introductions are often written first and what the writer is doing is warming up for the task ahead, but at the same time thrilled that they are knocking out words towards the word count.

Conclusions often emerge from the actual process of writing — which is great. If they do, this will often make the overall work feel much more coherent. If you keep a notebook alongside you as you write, then you can jot down what you think should be in your conclusion, for when you get there. When eventually you do decide on a conclusion, don't forget that it is not the time to introduce new material. No matter what kind of document you are writing, a conclusion should be based on the main body of the text. In an essay, the conclusion should summarise your argument. In a report, the conclusion should summarise the findings. The report-writer will also often be expected to come up with either a set of recommendations as to what the organisation should do next, or a series of ideas for discussion at your next exciting, unmissable, thrill-a-minute meeting.

If you also need an executive summary, as you might with a lengthy in-house management report, now is a good time to do it. Remember, an executive summary should normally take no more than one page, perhaps two if the report is unusually long. It should be pithy and precise. If you're not sure how to do it, there are several books that deal specifically with writing for business, although your company or institution may have a house style.

Editing for Voice, Meaning and Style

Now you are ready to look at the way in which you've written, rather than the actual content. Editing for style will include:

- Reducing verbiage
- Altering words, phrases and sentences
- Improving your tone and style
- Looking for fresh alternatives

This is the fun part. This is where you can start using all those techniques we'll look at later in the book.

Again, if you can leave a gap between your re-draft for content and this next editing stage, then so much the better. You can never underestimate the advantage of leaving a piece of writing to one side for a few days. Even if you're on a crazy deadline, at least putting in a lunch-break, or leaving the work overnight is more effective than ploughing straight on.

You're probably better off pruning unnecessary verbiage before you start putting on the style, but it is often difficult to do the two separately. Indeed, to be honest, you're almost bound to have made some stylistic revisions before you get to this step.

The best way to check through what you've written is to read it out loud. This sounds a bit tedious and, if you work in a shared office, might be impossible. Some modern text-processors offer text-to-speech, so you can always listen through headphones. It is easily the best way to check if what you've written sounds OK. You'll soon find out which sentences are too long and need dividing. You'll spot the nonsensical phrases, the gibberish and the non-sequiturs.

What to Look for (Once you've Sorted Your Overall Structure)

Sentence Structure:
- Linkages between paragraphs that don't make sense
- Sentences that don't make sense
- General clarity

Long-windedness, e.g.:
- Overlong sentences
- Padding/tautology/stuff that needs pruning
- Latinate words such as *terminate, transformational, potentiality*

Poor Word Choices, e.g.:
- Jargon, especially inappropriate jargon
- Dire management-speak, such as *actioned, blue sky thinking, thinking outside the box, baseline, coterminous, impact* (as a verb), *fast-track* (as a verb), *meaningful dialogue, slippage, tranche, delivery* (unless you're actually transporting something)

- Clichés – *children at X school are pleased as punch (unless they've put on a Punch & Judy show and you're writing a local newspaper article)*
- Weak verbs – *the house is/the river is ... the house stands, the river lies*
- Too many adjectives and adverbs
- Passive voice
- Badly-judged tone: Failing to talk to the reader in the way expected for the writing medium (e.g. too matey or too formal)

Once you've done all this, read your work out loud again. Ask someone else for a second opinion, this time asking them to check the style.

At this point, you could spend the rest of eternity trying to improve your work. Oscar Wilde is supposed to have once said that he spent the morning taking out a comma to see how a sentence sounded without it, and then spent the afternoon putting it back in. At some point, you have to say that the job is done, even if you would still like to fiddle with it. You now have to accept that your work is ready for its next step, that of checking for typos and other mistakes: proofreading.

Step 5 – Proofreading Your Work

The penultimate step for any document, before you start formatting and deciding on layout and so forth is proofreading. Proofreading is a hard job. There are people who are paid to do it for a living. Their trick is not to become absorbed in what they are reading, but to deal with the surface of a text.

At proofreading stage, you really should have established that what you're doing is picking over a manuscript looking for little errors. This shouldn't be the point at which you start to make wholesale changes or you'll just need to check what you've written yet again.

If You Wrote It, Get Someone Else to Proofread (If Possible)

It's extraordinarily difficult to check your own work. The brain and eye conspire to make you think that everything's fine when it isn't. This is not you being useless, it's just the way it is. We read what we think we've written.

If you do have to proofread your own work, a simple way of doing it is to read it aloud, as we have seen. Of course, this isn't always practical. Bellowing the contents of a confidential report in an open-plan office is a shortcut to the dole queue.

Don't Rely on the Spell or Grammar checker

Your word-processing app is great at putting little coloured lines underneath words or phrases the computer thinks are problematic. But, computer grammar checkers are unreliable and incapable of understanding subtleties of meaning. They also give you messages using such arcane grammatical terminology that you need a PhD in linguistics to understand them.

In fact, most of the mistakes we make are silly little ones, such as typing the word *form* for the word *from* and vice versa. I do it all the time. I also type *fro* instead of *for* a lot. These mistakes are caused by my incompetence as a self-taught typist. The fingers come down in slightly the wrong order. However, *fro, for, form* and *from* are all perfectly good words. The spell-checker is entirely happy with them. Then, when you come to read them, because these are such insignificant little words that act as simple connective tissue, your eye just goes straight across them and you're back in the trap of reading what you think you've written.

You've probably come across this poem which was doing the rounds of offices way back in the days when people would pass on photocopies to their friends in pubs:

A Little Poem Regarding Computer Spell Checkers

Eye halve a spelling chequer
It came with my pea sea
It plainly marques four my revue
Miss steaks eye kin knot sea.

Eye strike a key and type a word
And weight four it two say
Weather eye am wrong oar write
It shows me strait a weigh.

As soon as a mist ache is maid
It nose bee fore two long
And eye can put the error rite
Its rare lea ever wrong.

Eye have run this poem threw it
I am shore your pleased two no
Its letter perfect awl the weigh
My chequer tolled me sew.

OK, so we're probably not as bad as that, but point made. And now we have predictive text, which is the same problem, but moved to the start of each word you write rather than to be done at the end of the whole piece.

Schedule Enough Time

Proofreading is an important job, not an optional extra. You need real time to work on a manuscript properly. It's far too easy to skimp on this step. Often, this is the writer's fault, rather than the person doing the proofreading. If, for instance, you have 10 working days in which to write a report and you are relying on a colleague to proofread it, then you don't want to be passing it across for proofreading at lunchtime on day 10. You can sort this one out by making your writing deadline a couple of days before the handing-in deadline, for instance on day seven. Of course, this can go awry, but the point is that if you don't allow enough time for proofing, then you could end up with a slipshod job full of typos and other mistakes. These kinds of errors imply that you don't care about what you've written and undermine all your hard work. Leaving a gap means that you are more likely to see what you have written as though reading it for the first time. If you have to proofread your own work, put it aside for as long as you can. Even if that gap is just one hour, you will spot more bloopers than if you do it straight away.

Check Uncertainties against Reputable Sources

Have a useful library of dictionaries, thesauri, grammar and punctuation guides to hand. Don't assume that what you find on the Internet is correct. In fact, the Internet is stuffed with bad examples of almost everything. There's a list of useful books at the back of this one. It may be worth investing in some of them.

Print out Your Work for Checking

It's not enough to try to check your own work on-screen. Sure, it might be fine for picking up some obvious problems, because some of what you've written may have coloured lines where the word-processing programme has spotted a problem. But printing out your work automatically puts it into a different format, one that feels less familiar, and so you are more likely to spot mistakes. Working on paper also allows you to make revision marks easily against the text. Yes, I realise that these can be inserted electronically, but paper is usually quicker and more effective. The modern method of being able to share documents on screen for checking causes as many problems as it solves.

Always print your work out double-spaced and with good margins where you can fit in corrections. Use a good-sized font (12 or even larger). Try not to print on the reverse of anything, to reduce the possibility of confusion. If you do want to re-use printer paper, use it as a scrap pad, or stock-pile it, so that you're at least not printing out your latest version of a document on an earlier version of the same work.

Make Corrections in a Red Pen

Yes, red ink is nasty and rude and a bit schoolteachery, but it is highly visible. Only do this for your own work. It's rude doing it to other people's writing.

Proofread When You Are Fresh

If you find that you're working late to get a job finished and then you decide that you're going to proofread before you go home, then don't. Best leave it till the morning, if you can. The more tired you are, the less likely you are to be able to see what's really in front of you. Your mind will revert to the trick mentioned earlier. You will read what you think you've written, not what is actually on the page.

Avoid Interruptions

I know what you're thinking. Who is this man kidding? How do I field phone calls, deal with email, breast-feed the triplets and placate an irate boss whilst proofreading without interruptions?

It's not always feasible but do your best to find a quiet place where you won't be disturbed. Get yourself a cup of coffee and a red pen. Don't play music unless it is lyric-free. Don't play spoken-word radio. Shun the company of loud and boisterous people. See if your boss will let you do it at home, or if you're working at home, take yourself off somewhere else, such as a café, where the hubbub is generally just in the background.

Take breaks to aid your concentration. With all this coffee drinking, you'll probably need to. Divide your proofreading into sensible chunks. Read that chunk, then go off and do something else completely different, preferably something that doesn't involve looking at words. You could try the method of reading backwards so that you don't get distracted by the flow of meaning. It may also be worth making a checklist of your frequent mistakes and looking for them.

Use Marks in the Margin

Nobody expects you to be able to use proofreaders' marks, but one of the reasons for printing out with generous margins was so that you could write in them. Always put some kind of mark in the margin as well as in the text, that way you can easily spot the mistakes when you're tidying up the manuscript later on. It's also a good idea to put a massive, spidery asterisk at the top of every page where there is a mistake. That flags it up when you come to make changes.

And, on Your Final Run:

- Check arithmetic, equations, scientific symbols, etc. If you don't understand them, find someone who does
- Check your facts. Even ones you think you know
- Check the spelling of names — is it Davis or Davies? Do any foreign names (or words) need accents?

- Check phone numbers, addresses, dates, times, places and test out URLs by pasting them into your web browser and seeing if your computer takes you there. Get someone else to read them out to you if that makes life easier
- Make sure that any diagrams, illustrations, graphs, photographs, etc. have the correct captions and that any references in the text (e.g., *see figure 1*) correspond to the correct diagram
- Check headers and footers. Make sure that they are in a font consistent with the main body of the document.
- Make sure you've now got page numbers if you're going to have them. It's not a bad idea to set the page number up for the middle of the footer, that way it's in the same place if you print out your work on a duplex printer
- Expand or explain any abbreviations that you think might be beyond the knowledge of your readers

Last of All

Assuming you're not going to do any fancy desk-top publishing, take your contents page and put in the relevant page numbers. Then double-check these with a colleague or friend.

Have a cup of tea and a handful of chocolate digestives. You deserve it. Isn't proofreading boring?

Step 6 Presenting your work

How you present your work will depend entirely on what you're doing. However, for most general documents that don't require fancy publishing, here is a useful guide for A4-size printing:

Margins

Allow yourself around 3.5 cm (1½ inches, you oldsters) around all four edges. You can set this up on most word-processing apps. This means that anyone reading a print-out of your document has plenty of space in which to write comments. Yes, this can be done with shared documents on-screen, but paper beats a computer monitor every time.

Fonts

Basic fonts are best. Good old standards, such as Times New Roman, Garamond or even Arial do the job perfectly. Use the same font for headings as well, even if you go for larger size or bold. Use size 12 for the body of your text unless you need it bigger, for example for people with eye-sight problems.

Fonts that are supposed to look like handwriting are used by people who think that the reader might actually be stupid enough to mistake a printout for something genuinely personal. Avoid using them unless you want your tragic delusions to be trumpeted to the world. They don't make you a warmer human being. Similarly, Comic Sans doesn't make what you write funny. However, Comic Sans size 14 on a yellow/gold paper is often used for people with reading difficulties.

Headings

Decide on a size for titles/headings and sub-headings. I normally centre titles, but have any sub-heads justified to the left-hand margin. It doesn't matter too much, but it is best to be consistent.

Spacing

Use double-spacing. You can set your word-processor to do this automatically. Don't double-space by hitting the return bar.

If you're including a quotation of a few lines from another source, then it's best to indent the lines further and have single spacing.

Paragraphs

Indent the first line of any new paragraph except for the first one in any section, which should simply be left-justified. You should avoid using the right-justify setting (having the right-hand margins lined up neatly) as this means that the letters are spaced out to reach the end of a line, which can make reading slightly awkward. No, it's not neater.

Paper

Normally any office-standard 80 gsm paper is fine for a laser printer, but if you are using an inkjet, you may need to check to see how much the ink bleeds into the paper. For a while, I used the cheapest paper I could find for my laser printer, but now buy slightly better quality and seem to get fewer paper jams and less dust. You don't need ultra-posh, bond/woven/ laid paper or a weight of 100 gsm unless you're really trying to impress.

3

A Potted History of English

Languages rarely spring up fully formed. True, there are some invented languages, such as Esperanto or Klingon, but natural languages evolve. The English language is the result of centuries of development, some of it entirely illogical.

Towards the end of the 14th Century, Geoffrey Chaucer published his famous *Canterbury Tales*. It's often held to be the first example of a work written in anything resembling English. This is how it starts:

Whan that Aprill with his shoures soote
The droghte of March hath perced to the roote,
And bathed every veyne in swich licour
Of which vertu engendred is the flour;

This is Middle English. It's not the same language we use today, but several words are recognisable. The words *March*, *bathed*, *every*, and *which*, for instance, have not changed at all. Some words don't seem too far off current English usage: *Aprill, shoures, roote, virtu, flour*. We can make a fair stab at their meaning. You would be tempted to think that *soote* would be *soot*, but alas it means *sweet*, so there may be other traps too. Unless we're used to Middle English, it's not easy. However, if we concentrate and perhaps read it through a couple of times, we can probably disentangle enough to say that these few lines are about the arrival of spring showers.

A great deal has changed in the 600-plus years since Geoffrey unfurled his scroll and sharpened his quill. It's impossible to 'preserve' a living language. Yes, we can keep languages alive, as has been shown in the case of Welsh, which had been under threat for centuries. However, language changes all the time. English, as we use it now, is not an end-product; it's just where English happens to be at the time at which I am writing. Drop back a few years and the language is different. Just think how strange, and often downright difficult, reading Victorian novels seems to us only 150 years after they were written.

Some of these changes are down to the way our lives are altered by technology. Chaucer's pilgrims would not have put their feet up at the Tabard Inn, Southwark, and watched television, whilst idly texting on their smart phones.

Language also changes in other, subtler ways. Words shift their meaning. If I use the word *terrific* to describe something, I am singing its praises.

She made a cake and it was terrific.

But *terrific* originally meant something that was *terrifying*. If I'd used the same sentence to anyone before the middle of the 19th Century, they'd assume that the cake was so bad it caused fear amongst the teatime guests.

We are also left with words that are essentially meaningless in today's world. When did you last use a *penknife* for its real purpose, to cut yourself some nibs into quill pens? Nowadays, a penknife is probably a pocket-knife with a folding blade. *Rock 'n Roll* may describe a kind of music with a steady 4/4 beat, but the original phrase was jazz musicians' slang for sex. When Chaucer used the word *quaint*, he wasn't describing some cutesy Cotswold village with thatched cottages. Look it up. I'm far too polite to tell you.

There are, of course, fabulously wonderful words that drop out of use and you just sometimes wish they hadn't. A *goliard* is a glutton, a *mumpsimus* is a pedant, a *glister* sounds like it should be some glittering jewel, but is, in fact, an old term for an enema. A *fribbler* was a man who was head-over-heels in love with a woman, but whose infatuation was not enough to make him commit to marrying her.

Then there are the spellings that lose all contact with their original pronunciation. That *penknife* shares its roots with the French word *canif*, so at some point, we would have pronounced that first letter K, just as we would have done with *knee* (from the German *Knie*). Yet we still keep that silent K – another tricky spelling.

We also introduce words from other languages. *Bungalow, catamaran, chutney, loot, kedgeree, khaki, gymkhana, pyjamas, thug* and *shampoo* come from Indian languages, imported when the British liked to own vast tracts of the earth's surface.

Robot is a variation of the word *rabota*, which appears in several Eastern European languages, and usually means forced labour that was done by a serf to pay for their use of the land they farmed. The word was coined by a Czech playwright, Karel Capek.

Schadenfreude and *Zeitgeist* are more recent German imports. Obviously, English is stuffed with Germanic words. In this case, we seem to have adopted the words because there is no English word to do the job. *Schaden* means harm or damage and *Freude* means joy or pleasure. The whole word means *taking pleasure in someone else's misfortune*. For instance, if someone we really disliked had picked the winning lottery numbers, but lost the ticket, we might feel a little frisson of *Schadenfreude*.

Drinkers are supplied with plenty of foreign words. *Whisky*, unsurprisingly, comes from Gaelic, *Vodka* from the Russian, *Cognac* is an area of France that gives its name to a kind of brandy. *Sherry* and *Sangria* are Spanish.

It's not just drink. Often if we don't have our own word to describe a particular item, we just bring in the word. *Kimono* is a Japanese word. We also have a good number of recent-ish imports from French, such as *chic, croissant, savoir-faire, je-ne-sais-quoi* and *ambulance*.

Amen, as used at the end of prayers is from either the Greek or the Hebrew (or both), depending on which dictionary you check. It means *truth* or *certainty*.

Names also enter everyday use. We clean our houses with a *hoover*, write with *biros*, eat *Granny Smiths* and *Bramleys* and take rides on *Ferris wheels* whilst wearing our *trilbies*.

We even invent our own variations on words. After the Watergate scandal, the *-gate* suffix has been appended to other words, with the immediate implication that they involve a scandal. Watergate was fifty years ago, so it also shows how we cling to things. Since then, we've had *Irangate* and later on *Partygate*. It's hard to know how long these stories stay in the public consciousness as news stories come and go (remember *Cheriegate*?), but the *–gate* clings on. I look forward to the investigation into the founder of Microsoft's way of walking, which will become *Gatesgaitgate*.

We have a long history of doing this. All languages do it. Indeed, the French have their own organisation, the Académie Française, which stands sentinel over the wholesale importation of foreign words. Over the years they've objected to such Anglicisms as *le weekend, le snob, le parking,* and *le footing*.

Many of the words that have crept into our language from overseas are comparatively recent imports. They don't fully explain the way in which English developed. For that, we need to drop back in time to when England was inhabited by around a million and a half scruffy natives, who were under the charge of a garrison of possibly 100,000 or more Romans and soldiers from their empire. Then, in the mid- fifth Century, a decaying Roman Empire began to subside. Its northern border, marked by Hadrian's Wall was no longer defensible, so the armies of Rome packed their bags and left. At this point, those scruffy natives, mainly Celts, spoke Celtic (pronounced with a hard-C, unlike the Glaswegian football club of the same name).

There had already been little sniping raids and mini-invasions, but once the Romans had retreated, the inhabitants were now at the mercy of full-blown invaders. First came the Anglo-Saxons and Jutes from Northern Europe. They spoke various Germanic dialects. From this melting pot arose a language called Old English. One or two words are still recognisable today. From the Lord's Prayer, for example, words such *faeder, heofonum, todaeg, forgyf* are just about recognisable as early version of *father, heaven, today* and *forgive*. When the Norse invaders from Scandinavia came along, they too spoke Germanic languages, which meant that the existing language and the new language melted into one. Indeed, the experts who try to trace word derivations, etymologists, are often hard put to determine whether some words are derived from Anglo-Saxon or from Norse.

Despite a handful of words bearing similarities to modern English, the language was still nowhere near what we use today. The underlying grammar system involved a lot of complicated word endings. Grammarians refer to this as inflection. If you've studied German or Latin, you may know that words change according to their function in a sentence. They do in other languages too. For example, in French, the verb for *love* is based round the root word of *aim-*. *I love* is *j'aime*, but *we love* is *nous aimons*.

There's not a great deal of this left in modern English. We have such examples as *who* and *whom*, *they* and *them*, *he* and *him*, and of course plurals are a form of inflection (you're showing that there's more than one, normally by adding an -s). We also have it left over in our verb systems – *love, loved, loving, loves*.

When the Normans invaded in 1066, they colonised the country at breakneck speed. Within a couple of decades, William the Conqueror (who up until then had been plain William the Bastard and felt he needed a name change) doled out captured lands to his acolytes. He also set up a more modern system of government (*gouvernement*), and with that came a whole set of expressions that have stayed with us in many ways. The language of parliament (*parlement*) and the law (*loi*) is stuffed with Latinate terms, because French, unlike Anglo-Saxon, is derived from Latin. The Latinate words that we have, such as *nation, state, politics, policy, minister, legal, administration*, aren't a hangover from the Roman invasion of around 2,000 years ago. These words derive from Norman French. Many of us oldsters were sold the lie that Latin was at the root of all languages. Of course, we were told this by Latin teachers, desperate to hang onto their jobs in a modernising world. No, most of the longer words that end in *-ment, -ation, -ssion, -ant, -ance, -ence* come from the Normans.

This divide in language between Norman French and Anglo-Saxon is noticeable when it comes to food. It was the job of the ruling Lords to hold banquets and eat vast quantities of the stuff. The peasanty, knuckle-dragging Anglo-Saxons had to hunt the poor beasts down for their effete, land-grabbing masters. As a result, when the animal is on the hoof, we use a term derived from Germanic languages. As soon as it's on the menu, we use words that are often derived from the Norman French. A cow (*Kuh*) becomes beef (*boeuf*) as soon as we've spit-roasted it. The same happens with a hen (*Huhn*), which becomes a pullet (*poulet*); deer (*Tier* is the German word for any animal) is converted into venison (*venaison*) and so forth.

There were also still huge regional variations in the few hundred years that followed the Norman invasion, but as London became dominant, the London way of pronunciation became transferred onto paper. Then, largely between 1400 and 1800 came *The Great Vowel Shift*, a massive change in the way certain vowel-sounds were pronounced, which meant that the original spellings of words, which may have previously been related to their pronunciation, now no longer were. Bummer.

When Chaucer wrote about his pilgrims, we're beginning to get something that resembles modern English. By the time of the King James Bible, which was produced in 1611, the language is much more recognisable to us (and the language of that version of the Bible is gorgeous if you don't know it). However, those of you who have studied Shakespeare, writing at the same time, will know that whilst we can easily recognise this as being the same language, it doesn't necessarily make it easy to understand.

A great deal of written English was, of course, aimed at an educated elite. It was only over the intervening centuries that Sunday schools, then basic schools providing elementary education, began to spread literacy. Even in the 1750s, only a third of brides and two-thirds of bridegrooms were able to sign the marriage register in English Churches. The rest marked it with a cross. Signature illiteracy did not mean they couldn't read as it's not really until towards the end of the Victorian age that the actual process of writing (as differentiated from reading) was widely taught. Writing, the actual scribing of words on paper, was seen as a vocational skill. The children of the poor might increasingly be able to read, but ink and paper were expensive commodities.

English begs, borrows and steals. It is the ultimate hybrid language. It corrupts words, changes meanings, brings in new degrees of subtlety. Fashions for spellings come and go and differ between Anglophone countries and continents (*colour/color*). It is constantly evolving. There are brilliant differences, even if we just stick with food and drink again. Australians have *tinnies* and *barbies*. Americans eat *grits* and have their eggs *over-easy* or *sunnyside up*.

What a fabulous language this is. But why the little history lesson? What I hope to show is that it's hard to pin a living language down, that you can't preserve it in aspic, that writing English is not so much juggling with jelly as juggling with stinging jellyfish. English is hard, but it's not always hard-and-fast.

4

How to Give Your Writing Zip

This section is about positives and negatives. We're going to look at techniques that will help you write good, plain English as well as some of the traps to avoid. But let's be upbeat first of all and look at constructive ways of making your writing sound as good as possible.

We need to make sure we get the fundamentals right. You may ask why grammar, spelling and such actually matter? Surely, it's fine if we can understand what the writer is trying to say?

No, it isn't. Whilst occasional sloppy writing and typos might be taken with a pinch of salt, there are stories about shoddy communication skills amongst employees in the press all the time. They are often accompanied by estimates of how poorly written English costs the economy dear. The arguments for the cause of this rage on. School teachers, already near-broken by successive government 'initiatives', are held responsible. Parents are to blame. The government is to blame. Poverty is to blame. There's not the space here to chase down these arguments. Let's just say that good, plain English benefits your career prospects, the outfit you work for and the general economic well-being of the country.

I also think that a fundamental reason why we should try

to write good prose is that we can be proud of it. Do anything well and you get a sense of pride. People who lower their golf handicap, make their own Christmas cards, grow beautiful flowers and tasty vegetables get pleasure from a job well done. There's no reason you can't get the same kick from the written word. To paraphrase Matthew Arnold, if you've got something to say, you may as well say it as clearly as you can.

Develop Good Reading Habits

One of the best ways of developing your writing is by reading as much as you can. The more you read, the more you will begin to understand, even subconsciously, what makes the best writing. Try to develop two main reading habits:

Read critically. Try to understand why a piece of writing works or why it doesn't. Look for good writing as well as bad writing. To begin with, you may find the bad easier to spot than the good. It's a bit like service in a restaurant — it's easier to spot when it's incompetent. After a while, you'll be able to work out why pieces that command your attention do so.

Expand your vocabulary. If you're unsure what a word means, look it up. This is important not because you can then use large, impressive words, but so that words are more readily at your disposal. It increases your easily recalled vocabulary.

It doesn't matter what you read — thrillers, magazines, newspapers, non-fiction, instruction leaflets or the back of your breakfast cereal packet. Read anything and everything. Eventually, you should try to develop a taste for the best in whatever genre or medium you favour. The better the material you read, the more you will develop your vocabulary and sense of what works well. This is not a question of snobbery. There are hundreds of writers who produce accessible work that is well written. You don't have to fall back on an adverb-laden, cliché-ridden airport novelette. Or if you do, work out why it's so bad. Remember that there is often little correlation between a book's sales figures and the quality of writing between its covers. As Don Marquis said, 'If you want to get rich from writing, write the sort of thing that's read by persons who move their lips when reading to themselves.'

Write as Much and as Often as You Can

If you want to run a marathon, you don't just turn up on the day with an old pair of tatty trainers, having spent the previous six months slumped on the sofa washing down family packs of crisps with sugary soft drinks. Apply the same logic to your writing. Flexing your writing muscles makes the whole process a great deal easier. You'll also begin to learn your strengths and weaknesses as a writer. You'll find out if you fall into the category of canny planner or bash-on-and-see-what-happens. You'll find out if you work best in a bustling office or at your dining table. You'll know which phases of writing you find hard and which you find a breeze. You'll know how accurate you are on first draft and how many subsequent drafts you need to make.

As you write, you'll also discover which phrases you tend to overuse and you'll start to push what you write. Writers, even top-notch poets and novelists, rarely talk about their art. They talk about craft. You can improve your craft with practice.

Develop a Range of Different Styles and Tones

The way in which your 'voice' comes across is going to differ enormously depending on what you are doing. You don't want some kind of serious management report that might be dealing with millions of pounds' worth of business to sound like a chatty email to your drinking pal. Certain types of writing, obviously, demand more formality than others. A formal style doesn't have to be pompous. However, the kind of range of language you need for an essay is different from what you'd use in a text message to a mate. Knowing when to use what kind of language is vital.

Build a Relationship with Your Reader

Have you ever bought a piece of flat pack furniture? After three days struggling with the parts, you decide that it might be worth reading the instructions after all. You unfold them and they snarl at you. What you want is pleasant, gentle advice on how to put these shelves together and you get terse, shouty sentences that sound like a Vietnamese-War-era drill sergeant with a set of hapless recruits. Besides which, you're not sure what a flange control lever even looks like, let alone how you can turn it clockwise, especially if you need to tuck the chuffle under one arm at the same time as holding the counterbalancing screw.

The writer of these instructions has failed to build a relationship with the reader, which is why you have failed to build a set of shelves. Normally, the reader wants to feel as though the writer is on the same side as them. There are two little words that can do much of this work — *you* and *we*. If you use the word *you*, you are addressing the reader directly. It feels as though you're having a conversation with them. If you use *we*, then you are including the reader.

Think about Your use of Jargon

Baffling the reader is a big turn-off. If you can't explain something without resorting to jargon, you probably don't understand it yourself. Essentially, you ought to be able to explain most things to an intelligent 14-year-old without too much jargon and be capable of explaining the jargon you use. There is nothing wrong with jargon. All jobs have their own vocabulary, but it has to be used in its place.

Keep jargon for when you're writing for other specialists. For instance, if you're writing a computer manual for people who work constantly with computers, it would be a little bit insulting to start explaining to them what the monitor is. (*It's the one a bit like a telly screen, love, have you got that OK? Oo, you do catch on quickly.*) However, if you were to explain computers to people who are completely new to the subject, then you can't take too much of this vocabulary as read. They may understand the word *monitor*, which is becoming redundant anyway as laptops take over the world, but what about terms such as *CPU, hard disk drive, Ethernet* or *operating system*?

This is all part of understanding your reader. If you have any doubt about jargon, leave it out, or if necessary, provide a jargon-buster.

Gain the Reader's Confidence

The reader will normally have confidence in you until you mess up. I once managed to write an article that placed Stourport on the River Stour. Well, it makes sense doesn't it? Besides the information was just a snippet in passing. However, had I looked carefully at Stourport's full name, which was in large letters at the entrance to the town, I would have realised that it is actually called Stourport-on-Severn, which would have stopped irate readers writing to the magazine demanding my entrails be spread the length and breadth of Worcestershire. Why should they trust the meat of the article, the important bit, when I can't get something as simple as this right? Checking small facts is more than just useful, it's vital for the reader's confidence in you.

Write Positive Statements, Not Negative Ones

Writing positive statements makes sure the reader can easily understand what you have to say. What do sentences such as the following mean?

It wasn't as though I didn't want to be there.

If I hadn't not known about it, I wouldn't have not been able to come.

Not writing negative statements is not the worst way of ensuring that your reader is not confused.

No, I'm not sure what they mean and I wrote them. As soon as the negatives begin to pile up, we have a lot to disentangle. This isn't a blanket ban on negatives. Occasionally, you might want to cushion what you're saying:

We are not going to meet our targets this year softens the blow in comparison with *We are going to fail to meet our targets this year.* In cases such as this, a little bit of negative writing can be useful.

Think about Sentence Length

If you bear all of these techniques in mind, then you should find that you have made your work much more interesting, vibrant and, above all, readable. Making sure your sentences are not too long also aiding readability. There are ways of checking to see how easy or hard what you've written is, using readability scores. Let's just have a look at the technical side of this for a moment.

Much of the early work in assessing readability took place in the USA in the 1920s and 1930s. By the mid-1940s, there were increasingly sophisticated formulae being developed, with much of the early work being done by Rudolf Flesch, whose name lives on in two tests that are still useful today – the *Flesch Reading Ease Test* and the *Flesch-Kincaid Grade Level Test*. Another popular test is the *Gunning Fog Index*.

Basically, all these tests use word and sentence length, and sometimes the sophistication of the words being used, to make their calculations. Some indices are more highly developed than others. Don't worry too much about how these scores are calculated. The main thing is to think about how you can use the kinds of data they produce to help your writing.

Most popular word-processing apps have the facility to include readability statistics along with a word count. These will vary from one program to another. However, most of them have some means of checking readability scores. I ran a statistical/readability checker on an article written for a writers' magazine. It gives the following information:

Counts:

Words	*1,122*
Characters	*4,935*
Paragraphs	*16*
Sentences	*71*

Averages:

Sentences per paragraph	*5.0*
Words per sentence	*15.7*
Character per word	*4.4*

Readability:

Passive sentences	*2%*
Flesch reading Ease	*66*
Flesch-Kincaid Grade Level	*7.9*

Let's take each of these in turn:

Counts

From the 'counts', I'm normally only ever bothered about the number of words, because the important information comes later. The word count is important as that tells me how much I've done (and how much I still have to do). A magazine editor will give you a word count. Editors want you to be within a handful of words of this as they know exactly what space they have.

You can probably safely ignore the other three counts, as the more important maths is done for you in the next two main headings.

Averages

The average number of **sentences per paragraph** is useful. I normally aim for 5 as a maximum, especially if it's an article for a magazine or newspaper. That's because papers and magazines tend to have narrow columns. Breaking up paragraphs more often means that you inject more 'white space' into an article. White space helps guide the reader's eye.

The **words per sentence** is perhaps even more important. For most writing 15-20 words per sentence is fine. If you want to make your writing particularly easy, then you could aim for around the 11-14 mark. However, there is a danger you can insult your reader through over-simplification. If you score above 20 on anything other than academic work, look to see where you can split a sentence. It's usually not hard to find where you've banged on a bit too long.

Characters per word. I tend to ignore this. You're better off if this reads no more than 5 or 6, unless you're writing something technical or academic that, of necessity, includes longer, more complex vocabulary.

Readability

Passive Sentences

I explain about passive and active sentences in the grammar section. I'm pleased to see that I haven't got too many passive sentences. I would only worry if the proportion was nearing 10%. As the grammar-checker is so unreliable, you can't be sure the text-processing app really knows what a passive sentence is, so take this with a pinch of salt.

Flesch Reading Ease

This is measured on a score up to 100. The higher the score, the more readable you are. A figure between 60 and 80 should be easy for a 12–15-year-old to understand. I normally aim to be in the 60s for general-purpose writing, but again this is a rule-of-thumb. In the case of my test article, the reader needs a reading age of between 13 and 15. I'm happy with that, as that fits the idea of the intelligent 14-year-old I mentioned earlier.

Applying the same statistical analysis to this book, a quick review of the chapter-in-progress tells me that I have 13.3 words per sentence. The *Flesch Reading Ease* is 69.5. The *Flesch-Kincaid Grade Level* is 6.8, so the reading age required is roughly 12-13. I can live with that. I hope you can. It will have all changed by the time the book gets into print, though.

The Gunning Fog Index

Running the chapter through an on-line *Gunning Fog Index* gives me a score of just under 9. Most popular novels score around 8-10. Serious newspapers score anything from 11-14. Highly academic work can be as high as 16-20. Anything around the 10 mark is fine for most purposes.

That's the technical side of checking your work. But do be aware of the computer's limitations. It's far better to develop a feel for what works best, and that only comes with practice.

Vary Your Sentence Length

Whilst it's generally better to write sentences that are not over-long, one of the skills of writing is variation. If you want to have immediate impact, or to pick up the pace of what you're writing, keep your sentences short.

She heard it before she saw it. The sound was pure evil...

Yes, we can feel the tension rising as the monster leaps out at her from the darkness. This is a technique you will come across in a good deal of thrillers (and more literary work too). It's also worth using shorter sentences for pure information:

Linz is the capital of Upper Austria. It has a population of around a quarter of a million.

If you want to slow down the pace at which someone is reading, then you can afford slightly longer sentences:

In Linz, they would like you to believe that Linzertorte is the oldest known cake in the world. It's a confection of lattice-work pastry, jam and nuts that has your arteries hardening even before you bite into it.

For most writing, the important thing is to mix it up a bit. This is how you might write it for a travel article (although I prefer the previous version):

Linz is the capital of Upper Austria. It's also home to the Linzertorte. Here, they would like you to believe that the Linzertorte is the oldest known cake in the world. That may be tourist guff, but it doesn't stop the Linzertorte from being tasty. Or potentially bad for you. It's a confection of lattice-work pastry, jam and nuts that has your arteries hardening even before you bite into it.

Be Specific

We saw early on how weasily writing looks if it just deals in vague generalisations. Psychologists have also found that when people lie they tend towards using generalisations, whereas when they are telling the truth, they give specific details.

Specific details also bring a piece of writing alive. If we describe a dress as simply *the red dress*, we are being vague. Is that dress crimson, scarlet, vermilion, claret, puce, burgundy, maroon, magenta, berry red, pillar-box red or cherry red? A woman wearing a puce dress will come across to the reader as completely different from one in a maroon dress. My post-lady wears red, but she's not a scarlet woman.

Use Examples to Illustrate Your Ideas

Examples are like little stories that make it easier for the reader to follow. Jesus realised that this was a good technique when he tried to explain his philosophy. He told stories that were examples of what he meant. These parables, such as that of the

Good Samaritan, have stayed with us even into the modern, secular age.

If you can think of a little story to illustrate what you mean, that's great. However, do be wary of the kind of naff story-telling that is open to ridicule. There's one dreadful tale of a child walking along the beach where hundreds of starfish have been washed up. The child begins to throw them back and soon others join in and start throwing all the starfish back until they're all saved — the moral being that you too can make a difference just by doing little things. Yuck.

Stories like this are going to spark off the desire for subversion amongst anyone in your office with the faintest whiff of intelligence. If you do choose little narratives, make sure that they are not repulsively sentimental. Similarly, a university-level essay may need examples to back up concepts, arguments, or assertions, but telling your examiner little anecdotes may not be the most credible way of proving that you are thinking at a deep enough level.

The Rule of Three

There is something extraordinarily satisfying about lists with three items. That's the truth, the whole truth and nothing but the truth. Speechmakers have known this for years. Even Julius Caesar, way back, is quoted as having said, 'Veni, vidi, vici,' — I came, I saw, I conquered. Jesus talked about faith, hope and charity and he should know, being part of the trinity of the Father, Son and Holy Ghost and having received gold, frankincense and myrrh as a birthday present.

Comedians also know that three is the magic number. They build up expectation with the first two elements of the joke and then the third element is the funny. Look for it next time you watch a comedian. Item three is the humorous one or at least the one that is different. This is ingrained in us from childhood, where our stories involve three bears, three pigs or three wishes. Even an ellipsis is three dots ...

Choose Great Similes and Metaphors

If you use similes and metaphors at all, now is a good time to think hard about them. The problem with most similes (and metaphors) is that they tend to fall into the trap of being clichés. *Cold as ice* is a simile, and a cliché. Often, when the simile is new, it seems fresh and insightful. *As much use as a chocolate fireguard* may once have had people chuckling at the idea of a fire screen melting into a brown puddle on the hearth, but it's now meaningless, because it has been used too often.

Use Wit to Enhance What You Write

If you go right back to our example of the M & S suitcase, the description of how it's tested is witty. No, it's not roll-in-the-aisles, laugh-out-loud funny, nor is it intended to be. But it does have a sense of humour about it. You can also see that bad writing often has an air of pomposity. (The older I get, the more certain I've become that people who take themselves seriously do so because no-one else does.)

Be Sparing with Your Adjectives

The brain of the typical modern reader is stuffed full of images from the cinema, TV, magazines and the web. Modern readers are largely intolerant of over-long description, especially descriptions of places. However, we still want some kind of signposting. If you do need to conjure up a scene or a person, then try to think of what is the precise, telling detail that could give the reader a sense of a person or place. For this, we need well-chosen adjectives or descriptive phrases.

For instance, the late Alan Plater's description of the Trevor Chaplin character in the *Beiderbecke Affair* was *Trevor always walks as if it's raining.* Can you see that in your mind's eye?

If you start piling up the adjectives, you weaken the effect. Mark Twain once wrote,

> 'When you catch an adjective, kill it. No, I don't mean utterly, but kill most of them — then the rest will be valuable. They weaken when close together. They give strength when they are wide apart.'

Take even a short extract, such as:

The path that went down to the shore was covered in moss and wet, slimy and slippery.

This is weak writing. *Wet, slimy* and *slippery* mean more-or-less the same thing. More effective would be:

The path to the shore was treacherous.

Or, if you want to keep the *moss* in there:

The mossy path to the shore was treacherous.

Vague adjectives, such as *beautiful, big, wonderful, marvellous, evocative* do little work for the space they occupy on the page.

He was a big man.

Do you mean big as in tall, big as in fat or big as in brave?

He filled the doorway.

Cut out Intensifiers Where Possible

Intensifiers are words such as *very, quite, extremely, remarkably, pretty, slightly* when used in conjunction with a main adjective. For instance:

*Tiddles was a **very** large cat.*
*Driving into the brick wall was a **pretty** stupid thing to do.*

Let's look at Tiddles first. *Very* is an intensifier. It intensifies the idea of *large*, so that we're not just talking about a *large* cat, but a *very large* cat. Normally, it's better to look for a single adjective that will do the job of both words. A better choice might be:

*Tiddles was an **enormous** cat*
*Tiddles was a **huge** cat*

In the example of bad driving, if we assume that the car accident was the driver's fault, you could argue that we're bringing a touch of mild irony by using *pretty stupid*. In that case, you could probably get away with the intensifier *pretty*. However, if what you genuinely want to say is that the driver was *moronic*, then say so (and let's trim up the sentence at the same time). Then we end up with:

Driving into a wall was idiotic.

Choose Powerful Verbs

Which of these two do you think sounds better?

*She **moved cautiously** along the narrow path,* or
*She **edged** along the narrow path?*

Most people, I suspect would go for *edged*. *Edged* is a verb that carries a lot of weight. It gives you a cinematic picture of what's going on. As much as anything, stirring verbs remove the need to use adverbs (there's an explanation of verbs and adverbs in the grammar section). Many writing pundits suggest that using adverbs is bad style. That's debatable. If someone is *forcibly removed* from the premises, it's different from someone being *removed* from the premises. A blanket ban on adverbs is silly. However, getting the main power into a verb (the doing word) is a good technique and is something that you should aim to do. Take a sentence such as:

*The man walked **slowly** down the road.*

That *slowly* doesn't tell us anything. It's vague. If we pick a better verb, we can see far more clearly what is going on. Is this man injured? Or is he merely out for a breath of air? We don't get a picture of him if he's just being slow. However, if you choose something such as:

- *The man **limped** down the road*
- *The man **hobbled** down the road*
- *The man **strolled** down the road*
- *The man **sauntered** down the road*
- *The man **ambled** down the road*

These are much better choices. You've painted a picture in the reader's mind, or perhaps more accurately, shown the reader a little film of what the man is doing.

Use Simple Tenses Rather Than Compound Ones

This is a slightly tricky concept, but you'll probably remember something about this from language lessons at school. Imagine you've written something like this:

I used to walk to school with my brother every day. We used to take a packed lunch with us and when we got to school the teacher would give us each a small bottle of milk for break-time.

Nothing wrong with it as such, but it lacks a sense of immediacy. *Used to walk/used to take/would give* are all compound verbs, that is verbs made up of two or more words. They somehow distance the reader from the writing. Using simple, one-word tenses is a better ploy:

I walked to school with my brother every day. We took a packed lunch and when we got to school, the teacher gave us each a small bottle of milk for break-time.

And, yes, there are other things I'd like to do to this piece of writing to sharpen it up, but we're sticking with verbs for the moment. It's almost as though the more words in a compound verb, the more distanced the reader feels. What about this?

She had been wondering when he might be coming home.

That *she had been wondering* is particularly clumsy.

Here is a possible solution:

'When is he coming home?' she wondered.

It may not be possible to remove all compound verbs, but it's worthwhile looking at any you've written to see if they are punching their weight.

Use Active Verbs Rather Than the Passive

If you know what this means, skip ahead. If not, you may want to read up a little in the grammar section as well as reading this little section.

Normally, you're better off avoiding using the passive. When

I was at school, we had to write our science reports along these lines:

A Bunsen burner was used to heat the test-tube. When the liquid was heated to the correct temperature, it was poured into a glass beaker. The contents were measured to see if the amount of liquid had changed.

All of this uses the passive. I understand that it's no longer the fashion, so the modern school student is free to write:

We heated the test-tube with a Bunsen burner. Once the liquid was at the correct temperature, we poured it into a glass beaker. We measured it … etc.

In other words, you are now allowed to write up your reports in a much more personal way, largely using the active voice. You'll agree that it sounds friendlier, although the scientists amongst you will have noticed that whilst the bit about grammar may be OK, the science is dodgy.

To explain a little further, these sentences are in the passive:

*The job **was carried** out by a man with a pickaxe.*
*The postman **was bitten** by a dog.*
*The production line **was closed** for repairs.*

The first two examples are easy to change into the active voice:

*A man **carried** out the job with a pickaxe.*
*A dog **bit** the postman.*

There's nothing wrong with *The production line was closed down for repair.* Yes, it's passive, but it's a kind of general passive. Perhaps we can't say with any certainty who carried out the repairs, or it's irrelevant. It's fine to use the passive in these kinds of cases:

*He **was hit** by a car.*

We don't know anything more about the car. We can't be sure about the car.

I'm afraid the post of junior manager will be redundant on April 1st

The reality is that we're getting rid of you. But in this instance, if we use a more direct, plain English version: *I am making you redundant on April 1st,* it actually personalises the situation much more, even if it is the truth (although technically, you can't make a person redundant, just a job). The passive voice can, therefore, occasionally be handy. Use it sparingly.

Make It Concise

The French mathematician-philosopher Pascale once wrote, 'I have made this letter longer than usual because I lack the time to make it shorter.'

He had a point. It's often far more difficult to be brief and to the point than it is to waffle about a subject. As I've suggested before, it's often worth looking at the first few paragraphs of what you write, as this tends to be where we get too much flab because we're still warming up to our task. Sometimes we write material that is little more than literary throat clearing. Don't chide yourself if you find that you do this. It is possible that the only way you can get started is by doing this.

Use Anglo-Saxon Words, Rather Than Latinate Ones

Essentially, this means that you should choose more straight-forward words over more complex ones. There is a tendency to assume that long words make you sound clever. This isn't the case. Longer words can make you look pretentious, pompous or may even make readers think you've got something to hide. Of course, if you're writing about the law or government, you're inevitably going to have to use these kinds of words, but for most writing, the word *termination* does not sound better than the word *end*. If you want to *use* something, *use* it, don't *utilise* it. Don't use the word *property* when what you really mean is *house*, unless you are a property developer, or invest in property as someone might invest in the stock market.

Cut Unnecessary Words

Many of us have pet phrases that could easily be shortened. I often find myself typing some variation of the phrase *one of the best ways to do this*. Why not write *a good way to do this* or *one good way*? It's partly habit and also partly because when we try to sound friendly, we inevitably tend towards long-windedness. The same habit that has us write *in order to* instead of *to, bring to a conclusion (end)* and *at this point in time (now)*. Whenever you find yourself writing:

   This will provide us with the potential to ...

Stop immediately and write something pithier instead:

   We will be able to/This will let us ...

There's a whole long list of these later in the book.

Redundancies and Repetitions

It's extremely easy to write the same thing twice, often in two different ways. The posh word for saying the same thing twice, but in different ways is tautology.

It was 8 a.m. in the morning.

A.M. means the same thing as *morning;* you don't need both.

There was a tiny little kitten sitting on the doorstep.

Tiny may be smaller than *little,* but you don't need both.

'It's very difficult for me,' he shouted loudly.

Shouting is loud. There's no need to tell us that, as we know it already.

The fearless knight showed his bravery by boldly slaying the dragon.

Slaying dragons is an act of bravery, so we don't need to be told that he's *bold* and *fearless* as well. Let's just have one of *fearless, bravery* or *boldly.* Alternatively, you can big up the dragon.

Don't Confuse Your Reader

Make sure what you write makes sense. If you can't express clearly what you mean, then your readers are going to lose faith in you and start wondering if you know anything at all. This often happens when sentences run on for too long. They start to get saggy in the middle and you lose control. It happens to all of us.

Let's imagine you have to write a set of instructions on how to use the fancy new coffee-making machine. If you explain it to your colleague face-to-face and she doesn't grasp what you mean at any given point, she can ask you to stop and go over it. You then have the opportunity to re-word what you've just said and to demonstrate which buttons need pressing and how the jug fits on the hotplate. That second chance isn't there with the written word. You need to be clear first time.

In the past, I've often had students explain the meaning of convoluted sentences that they've written, but I've failed to disentangle. 'I know what I mean,' they say. I have no doubt they do. But I don't, and I'm the reader. They have a duty of care to make sure that I can understand what they've written.

Don't Write Management Bollocks

It's the curse of the modern age: the empty verbiage that comes from the computer keyboards of barely literate managers. You know the kind of thing:

We need to upscale this project so that we add value to our offer.

Indeed, a poke around the web quickly reveals entire sites dedicated to ridiculing management-speak-gobbledygook. Some twaddle runs for breathless sentence after sentence. One major international company had the pithy, but meaningless *Solutionism stories – moving at the speed of small* on their website. Yes, your guess is as good as mine. Another declares:

Our experience has taught us that the key to realising wider benefits for our clients lies in taking a more complete view and developing comprehensive solutions that achieve long-term results.

I genuinely can't tell you what it means. And I don't suppose whoever wrote it can. It's just vaguely positive cant. I'm not even convinced it makes grammatical sense. Does it simply mean 'we do our job well'? On the same, gloriously appalling site, comes the following:

We operate across two broad operating segments: secure solutions and cash solutions.

What is an operating segment? Is it like an orange segment? Is an orange segment allowed to carry out operations? How would you like it if a slice of tangerine came up to you in your hospital bed and offered to take out your appendix? Is it a fully licensed doctor? Has it taken the Hippocratic Oath? And what's a secure solution? A key, a lock, a safety deposit box, the immediate imprisonment of people who write this guff?

In a desperate effort to sound positive (because sounding positive is so much better than being truthful as some politicians well know), the worst kinds of managers no longer deal with problems, but issues or challenges. Despite being intellectually challenged (or with issues surrounding intelligential capacity) themselves, they are so wrapped up in their reflective practice that they are capable of simultaneously blue-sky thinking, pushing the envelope of thinking, thinking outside the box, whilst undertaking 360 degree thinking and picking the low-hanging fruit.

Perhaps a self-awareness course would be useful.

Of course, anyone using phrases like these is doing no thinking at all. Anyone using these expressions is parroting ideas. They're the last person you'd want to go to for something fresh and original. In fact, the person thinking outside the box and through 360 degrees is possibly thinking in two dimensions at the same time. Here's one I made up. 'We need to move from two-dimensional to multi-dimensional thinking.' Try it at work. See if it catches on.

It would be interesting to find out how this kind of bizarre language has entered common currency and, for all the criticism it receives, how it still manages to flourish. For the moment, we can only guess at its causes, which I would suggest include:

- They genuinely don't know what they're talking about, which you can tell from the fact they're using this kind of nonsense language
- Fear of **not** using this kind of language – if everyone else in the organisation is using it, I'm going to appear an idiot if I write and speak plainly and clearly

- They think it impresses people. This is because they have no social awareness
- They think it impresses the boss. This beats being good at your job, which may take skill and hard work
- They have to have a good reason for earning what are often ridiculous sums of money
- They need to make up for not earning ridiculous amounts of money by sounding as if they do
- They don't give a damn about the people who work for them, so it's reflected in how they write, speak and think
- They've just got into the habit and can't help themselves
- They think it adds weight to the jobs they are doing. As though they're not important enough already
- If they use idiotic language like this, nobody with any real talent is ever going to want to be a manager, so they won't ever get shown up by people who might actually be able to do the job far better than they can
- All of the above …

I'm sure you can add reasons of your own, many of which may be less flattering, and will certainly use earthier language.

The worst thing about this kind of writing is that the person on the receiving end of it – the reader – switches off. We see meaningless drivel and it washes over us. If it does get any reaction at all, it is only the sort of angry rant such balderdash deserves. Meanwhile, these people get their ducks all in a row and never let the grass grow under their feet as they busy themselves actioning the incentivisation of co-colleagues, some of whom may also be stakeholders. They're too busy upscaling, cascading, renewing the pipelines and shifting the paradigm to stop and wonder at the absolute tripe gushing from their keyboards. Whilst we just want to make them coterminous with the fast lane of the M6.

Avoid Psychobabble

Some writing also seems to have been infected by playground-level psychology. Yes, we're referring to the dreaded psychobabble, which seems to be spreading.

He's in a bad place at the moment. No, he's not in a bad place. A war zone is a bad place. He's down in the dumps, or got the blues, or if it's clinical, he may be depressed.

This is part of our process of empowerment. We're letting you get on with the job. Normally, if they've used the word *empowerment*, they're telling you that you can get on with the job, but they're actually lying. You can have responsibility if things go wrong, but no credit if they go right.

The current workforce seems to be in a state of denial about the issues facing us.

We have failed to explain to the workforce what the real problems are.

There are relationship issues between the two of them.

They can't stand each other. Although you'll need to be a bit subtler if you commit it to paper or an email.

We're going to take a holistic approach to this.

No you're not.

Psychobabblers, like management-bollockeers, assume that the more important they sound on paper, the more important they will be seen by the reader. But readers don't want pomposity and verbiage; they want to understand what it is you are trying to say.

The psychobabblers also assume that vague positive statements make them sound good. It doesn't. Current research shows that CEOs who are lying tend to make overblown upbeat positive statements and ignore real specifics. I don't suggest for a single moment that this is what is going on with the websites

I pilloried. But if you want to engender consumer confidence, you need to let customers know exactly what it is you're good at.

Avoid Ambiguity

Try to make everything clear by avoiding ambiguous writing. For instance, a television interviewer asks a singer:

Have you always wanted to sing badly?

Does the singer sing badly? The interviewer surely means:

Have you always had a deep desire to sing?

You can find yourself in all sorts of trouble when you start using pronouns. Of course, there is the famous:

When I nod my head, hit it.

But it's also easy enough to know in your own mind what you mean, but confuse the reader.

Mary crossed the road to meet Penelope. She was very pleased to see her.
'How are you?' she asked.
'I'm fine,' came the reply.

If something could even remotely be misread, change it.

Avoid Clichés

Here come the hobbling spent forces that are the clichés. Here's a smattering that I come across, you will no doubt come across shiploads more of the sinister beasts yourself:

At the end of the day, engage with, outcome, add value, consultation, ethos, implementation, initiate, ensure, honour the pledge, delivery, platform, activity, stimulate, opportunity, impact (as a verb), *consensus, document* (as a verb), *journey* (stolen from the acting profession), *approach* ...

Don't use them.

Avoid Slang

Of course, there are times when you can use slang, but most formal documents are not the place for it. It's a pity, really, because slang provides us with some of the most colourful language that we have. It also dates remarkably quickly, as you spiffing, whizzo, hep cool cats know. It's best to reserve slang, alongside textspeak, emojis, emoticons and other less formal patterns of writing for use amongst friends.

Accidental Showing-off — The Big I-am

If you're writing about yourself, it's impossible to avoid using words such as *I, me* and *myself.* If you're not careful, what you see as being merely the recounting of a personal tale on paper can end up looking like the Carmen Miranda song, *I-I-I-I like you very much!* By the way, if you're too young to remember Carmen Miranda, check her out on the Internet. It's amazing what you can do with an entire fruit-bowl on your head.

One of the easiest ways to overcome the problem is to avoid using the word *I* at the start of a sentence, especially if that sentence is the start of a new paragraph. Instead of having *I* at the beginning, you move the sentence around so that it is embedded in the middle somewhere. For example, if your original sentence is:

I was going to the coast for the day when I bumped into an old friend.

You could re-write it as:

On my way to the coast, I bumped into an old friend.

Putting that *I* mid-sentence makes it look far less intrusive. You could also simply cut down on the frequency of the word *I*, so a sentence such as:

I think that I might look into this matter

is rewritten as:

I might look into this.

This version also has the added advantage of being concise.

If you can successfully substitute *we* for *I*, then that also reduces the likelihood of your writing being seen as egocentric.

Avoid Overstating the Case and Meaningless Words

Sometimes what we write can come across too strongly for other people. There are also words whose use has become essentially meaningless. If you use words such as:

Incredibly, fabulous, majestic, exciting, horrific, terrifying

They don't carry much weight as they have lost their original sense. If something is *incredible*, it should mean that it is *hard to believe*. Now, it's used as a variant of *very*:

The Titanic was an incredibly big ship.

Fabulous should mean that a story is the stuff of fables. It doesn't anymore. Words such as *exciting* don't make us feel excited. If you want to convey the excitement of something, look around for some way to describe that excitement.

I'm sure you could create your own list of meaningless words that are trotted out unthinkingly. Let me get you started with my own pet peeve: *evocative*.

Racist and Sexist Writing

It should be obvious that you want to avoid racist writing. However, it's not always as easy as you might hope. For instance, where once *coloured* was considered the non-racist term for people who are *non-white*, it has since developed derogatory overtones, probably due to its use in Apartheid South Africa. Similarly, *half-caste* might have once been acceptable, but it really refers to the caste system in parts of Asia and not the offspring of people with different skin tones. *Mixed race* is now preferred. It's also better not to use a vague term, such as *ethnic*, as everyone is ethnic. Morris dancing is an ethnic English dance form.

It's worth asking if we need to identify someone's race anyway. *He's a black policeman.* Is it actually relevant that he's black? Why? Perhaps it's relevant if he was set upon by racist thugs. It's also easy to make assumptions. Someone who is *American* could just as easily come from Brazil as the USA. Most of the time, a person's ethnicity is entirely irrelevant, so ask yourself why you're even mentioning it.

It's probably easier to avoid racist writing than it is sexist. There are so many set phrases and expressions that have entered the language that are inherently sexist, that it's easy to use them unconsciously without even considering any possible offence, when there are easy alternatives:

Manning the help desk	*staffing the helpdesk*
Man-made fibres	*synthetic fibres*
Man in the street	*general public*
The Old Masters	*classical painters*

What's more, English possesses no word that does the job of both *she* and *he* when we mean just one person. Perhaps the best solution is to plump for *they*. Grammatically, this is technically incorrect, but it works. Otherwise, we can end up writing:

The child should learn how to behave. **He** or **she** *needs to develop self-control.*

We've also got the same problem with *him/her* and *himself/ herself* — and indeed have I been inherently sexist by putting *him* before *her*? Here are four examples of essentially saying the same thing:

1. *A writer should take care not to make too many mistakes as this will reflect badly on him.*
2. *A writer should take care not to make too many mistakes as this will reflect badly on her.*
3. *A writer should take care not to make too many mistakes as this will reflect badly on him/her.*
4. *A writer should take care not to make too many mistakes as this will reflect badly on them?*

If you opt for the masculine *him* (1), you can fall into the trap of sounding sexist by excluding women. Obviously, women don't write at all. Nobody's ever heard of J. K. Rowling, Agatha Christie or P. D. James.

On the other hand, if you plump for *her* (2), you might come over as sounding a little strident. Look at me, I'm deliberately using *her* to show off that either I'm a feminist or I'm a New Age Man who understands all that stuff. Or, it could just be another case of undiluted sexism, especially if the sentence in question was *A cook should ensure she washes her hands before starting.* A cook? Obviously it's a woman.

Choose *him/her* (3) and it's plain clumsy. It's almost as if you're expecting us to cross one out as we might when filling in a form.

Them (4) is technically ungrammatical — *a writer* is singular, but *them* is plural. This is nit-picking. In this case, you could get round it by pluralising the word *writer*:

Writers should take care not to make too many mistakes as this will reflect badly on them.

Using either *they* or *them*, depending on which you need grammatically, seems fine. Besides, there is also a massive debate around gender identity at the moment, which also makes it easy to cause offence when none is intended. I asked a couple of literate friends what they thought and they agreed with this approach.

Don't Condescend to Your Reader

Just because someone may be new to a topic, doesn't mean they're entirely stupid. We know that if we throw in too much jargon, we can lose people. On the other hand, if we reduce everything we write to something that is too childish, then we stand a chance of alienating readers by treating them like morons. This is a fine line to tread and it's tough to get it right.

If you're not sure whether you're getting the tone and register right, produce a sample page. Then ask someone appropriate, such as a colleague or a friend with the same level of knowledge you'd expect from your reader, to give their opinion (a colleague … their!). Don't forget that whenever you ask someone else to read your work, you also need to explain to them what response you want from their reading.

If you have the happy knack of getting the tone, register and level right, then good for you. Few of us have that ability.

Avoid Static Description

If you're writing the kind of work that requires description, try not to give us the photograph or portrait of what you want us to see, but a cinema film. Back in 1900, when Jerome K Jerome wrote his follow-up to Three Men in a Boat, his preface included the following:

> *Lastly, in this book there will be no scenery. This is not laziness on my part; it is self-control. Nothing is easier to write than scenery; nothing more difficult and unnecessary to read ... An American friend of mine, a cultured gentleman, who loved poetry well enough for its own sake, told me that he had obtained a more correct and more satisfying idea of the Lake District from an eighteenpenny book of photographic views than from all the works of Coleridge, Southey, and Wordsworth put together.*

Given that we have film, TV and the Internet as well as Jerome's picture postcards, then we have to be far cleverer in our use of description than writers of a century ago. Yes, some people will drool over the opening of Thomas Hardy's Return of the Native, where he spends the first seventeen pages or so describing Egdon Heath, but most modern readers will find it heavy-going.

If you're describing people, as far as possible describe them in action. In his travel book, *A Tall Man in a Low Land*, Harry Pearson's description of the former professional cyclist Eddy Merckx shows how you can add movement to static description by using vivid verbs and a sprinkling of precise adjectives:

> *Nowadays Eddy Merckx is rotund to the point of globularity. Putting on weight is a problem for the retired pro cyclist. Riding burns up a lot of energy, and they eat accordingly; chomping down a 3,500-calorie breakfast is a hard habit to break. Once they slip off the saddle for the final time many bike-racers balloon up as if someone has just pulled the ripcord on a life-jacket beneath their shirt.*

Apparently, to be fair to Merckx, he has slimmed down since this was written. This is a description made more cinematic using words and phrases such as *chomp, riding, slip off the saddle, pulled the ripcord*.

Think cinema and keep that camera moving.

Brackets and Footnotes

Use brackets sparingly. Ask yourself if what you're saying is important. If it is, then why is it in brackets, or for that matter footnotes? Brackets are useful for explaining abbreviations and for occasional short side comments, but if you find you're using them too often, it might be an idea to see how you can incorporate what you're writing into the main body of the text.

Reading footnotes was once described as like interrupting your honeymoon to go and answer the door.[1] If it's not important enough to be in the main body of the text, why is it there at all? The only exception is academic citations. You may need to use a specific system. Harvard, for instance, is common. There are plenty of guides online and if you are studying through a formal institution, then you are likely to be given precise guidelines.

If you do need to use a referencing system for a non-academic assignment such as writing a management report, then you'll have to go with company policy. Opt for endnotes rather than footnotes if you can. These, obviously, come at the end of a piece of writing. They are generally the best method if you need to show your sources and whoever is paying you to write allows this system.

---

[1] See what I mean. Look at how annoying a footnote can be. It ruins the reading flow. You can go back to the main text now, which means re-tracing steps to where you were on the page.

Don't Bore Your Reader

Bored readers stop reading. This means that the huge amount of effort you put into writing has not paid off. It's a waste of time. Make sure that when you polish your draft for the final time, which we'll get to later, your prose sparkles.

Do this by putting into practice all the elements we've looked at. But most of all, get someone else to read what you have written to see if it all makes sense and engages the reader.

5

A Brief History of Grammar, Spelling and Punctuation

There is a scene in *Monty Python's Life of Brian* which must have rung bells with a generation of Latin-learners. Brian scrawls graffiti on the wall of the fort of the occupying Roman army. The graffiti is supposed to say *Romans Go Home* in Latin. He is caught in the act by an ear-twisting Centurion who forces him to correct his bad grammar, re-write the sentence correctly, and then copy it out 100 times.

In the old days, grammar was king. Accuracy was everything. This was fine for Latin, as it was no longer a living language; it was spoken only by priests and dead Romans. You relied on highly formalised patterns to learn 'rules'. You then applied these to your translations. I expect that even if you've never learnt Latin yourself, you'll probably know someone who can recite you *Amo, amas, amat, amamus, amatis, amant* (I love, you love, he/she/it loves, we love, you [plural] love, they love). For us oldsters, Latin was organised into tables and boxes.

Often what we learnt consisted of lists, such as the one above, of how nouns and verbs change (what grammarians call *inflect*), depending on their function in a sentence. Fair enough, once you get the hang of it, but this divorcing of the rules from any meaningful context meant that everything seemed highly theoretical at best and puzzling at worst. For instance, early on, you learn that *mensa (table)* can mean *Oh, table!*

Imagine the scene in the Latin lesson:

> *A Latin teacher, struggling with a vile, whisky-induced hangover, stares at his charges.*
>
> *'The vocative case, mensa, means* **oh table**.*' He pauses briefly to check in his pocket for mints to disguise his breath. 'Yes, Corder, what is it?'*
>
> *'When would you use that, sir?'*
>
> *'If you wanted to talk to a table.'*
>
> *'Did the Romans used to talk to tables, sir?'*
>
> *'Don't be so stupid, boy.'*

This ramming of dusty grammar down the parched throats of children happened in English lessons too and was inevitably going to result in a backlash. It all went out of fashion. A generation of schoolteachers, desperate to give their charges a better experience, began shifting the focus of their lessons. Eventually, like craft skills lost if not handed down the generations, grammar became some kind of distant discipline; as arcane as Middle English as relevant to the computerised classroom as Jethro Tull's seed drill is to modern farming. For a period between the 1960s and the 1980s, the teaching of English grammar fell out of favour in Britain.

Some teachers were not just grammar agnostics, but defiantly anti-grammar. In the early 1980s, I read a newspaper article written by a teacher, arguing that because a word such as *break* could be a noun (*we're on our* **break**) or a verb (*I'm going to* **break** *this stick in two*), it wasn't worth teaching grammar. This, of course, is as monstrously ludicrous as the child-thumping Latinists' exercises in torture. Grammar is all about context, as we shall soon see.

When the gnomes who fiddle with the education system decided they wanted grammar back, they were facing an uphill battle. Added to the difficulty of re-introducing the subject with teachers who hadn't been taught it themselves, furious rows now erupted. In one corner, there were those who thought grammar should tell you exactly how to write (prescriptivists); in the other, those who argued that grammar was a way of trying to explain what really happened in language (descriptivists). The battle became entrenched along vaguely political lines. Prescriptivists were somehow dyed-in-the-wool Tories, desperate to put the grammar back into grammar schools and the descriptivists, woolly liberal-minded *Guardianistas* who ate far too much muesli and wore socks with their sandals. Indeed, it still goes on. Of course, if you genuinely cared about language, you wouldn't use such ugly words as *prescriptivist* or *descriptivist*.

Stuck in the middle of this, as always, are the poor school-children of Britain (or perhaps more precisely England and Wales). Every year the press harangues them about how much worse they are than previous generations. The oldsters knew far more, could spell far better, were better prepared for the world of work and got along fine with just six old pence in pocket money. They then have a leviathan syllabus imposed on them by politicians who wouldn't last a fortnight teaching in a school classroom.

Most grammar doesn't actually have to be directly taught anyway. As we acquire language, we pick up the shape of grammar. We may not know its terminology, but by the time most of us get to primary school, we know there's something wrong if we say, 'give **he** the book' instead of 'give **him** the book'. This is fine for the spoken word. It gets a bit trickier when it comes to the written form of language, although there is an enjoyable way of absorbing written grammar, and spelling, and punctuation. It's called reading.

Read, and you accidentally learn the way language works. You may not be able to define what a noun or verb is, but you'll have a good idea of how to put a sentence together. More importantly, you'll be reading language that is being used to tell stories, entertain, impart facts, increase your knowledge, make you laugh and help you understand the world. Illustrative examples of grammar, as we shall soon see, are always little phrases and sentences that have no real context.

Punctuation – the New Kid on the Block

Punctuation is a reasonably recent addition to the tools at your disposal. It may not seem obvious, but the spaces between words are also a form of basic punctuation. If you ever see early tombs, you'll notice that the words of inscriptions run into one another, and even line-breaks are apt to come mid-word. The space between words makes them easier to read. A full stop tells us a sentence has ended. And what do you do when you come across a question mark? Yes, you spot that it's a question.

Like all conventions, punctuation, has taken time to grow into the present system and to complicate matters the system's changing all the time too. When Caxton first ran his printing presses, he used either a *slash* / or a *double-slash* // to indicate when it was time for the readers to catch their breaths before moving on. The idea that a comma, a colon and the full stop should be pauses of slightly different lengths dates from the 19th Century. And today, the semi-colon is falling out of favour as writers tend to prefer the dash –.

Look at most of our European neighbours and you'll find words which have additional marks attached to various letters:

Fräulein, idées reçues, mañana. You've probably come across terms such as cedilla, acute accent, grave accent, umlaut, tilde or circumflex at some point, but more useful information has pushed them out of your brain's store. We often refer to these little twiddly bits as accents, although more accurately, they should be called diacritical marks. English tends to use them less often than our cross-channel chums. Those English words that have these marks are normally either hangovers from older English or imports. If you want the word *blessed* to be pronounced with two syllables (*bless – ed* rather than *blest*), you should write *blessèd*. There are words adopted wholesale, such as *fiancé* or *cliché* from the French, which have acute accents. This means that you sound the *-e*, so that it's not *fianc* or *clich*.

We also have the tréma, which makes you separate out the vowel sounds (and apparently also means 'stage fright' in Serbian. Bless you, internet). In the names *Zoë* or *Noël*, that *ë* indicates that we need a new sound for the second vowel. Noël is pronounced *nowell* rather than *nole*. You may hear the mark above the *ë* in these examples referred to as an umlaut. Technically, that's wrong. An umlaut alters the pronunciation of the vowel it marks, whereas in a word such as *naïve*, we're indicating that you should sound the two vowels. By the way, the composer Handel is, more strictly speaking Händel, which means we should pronounce his name *Hendel*. Too late. We don't. Refer to him as Handel (handle) in Germany and they have no idea who you mean. On the other hand, the Germans can struggle over in Britain. I had a good ten minutes of fun once watching a German friend ordering a pint of Löwenbräu in a British pub. The barman was really confused as to why he was asking for *lervenbroy*, when he just wanted a *lowenbrow*. The town of *Lodz* in Poland is also a lot of fun to pronounce.

Bizarre Spelling: English Knows How to Confuse

Pronouncing Löwenbräu the German way might look hard, but once you've cracked the relationship between German spelling and pronunciation, it makes sense. The same can't be said of English, where the relationship between spelling and pronunciation often seems to have been invented by someone who was just out to make our schooldays miserable.

Maybe God is punishing us for having a stripped-down grammar system by landing us with a system of spelling that is, frankly, barmy. The phrase *Pacific Ocean* contains three different pronunciations of the letter 'C'. And if you're not convinced, just take a look at this. I found it on a website, although I've seen variations of it over the years and am sure it may already have done the rounds:

Rough-coated, dough-faced, thoughtful ploughman, John Gough, strode through the streets of Scarborough; after falling into a slough on Coughlin road near the lough (dry due to drought), he coughed and hiccoughed, then checked his horse's houghs and washed up in a trough.

How on earth could anyone teach a non-native speaker to pronounce that? In fact, how could you teach a native speaker of English with a fist-full of qualifications how that works? It's pure lunacy. On the other hand, at least it gives you a little game for you to play at your place of work. How many ways can your colleagues come up with of pronouncing the letter combination *-ough*. I list below what I think may be nine different ways.

Slough	*-ow*, as in the town.
Through	*-oo*, as in too.
Enough	*-uff*, as in huff.
Though	*-oh*, to rhyme with so.

Trough	-*off*, as in scoff.
Thorough	-*uh*, as in udder.
Thought	-*awl-or*, as in Thor.
Hiccough	-*up*, although some people argue that hiccough should be spelled hiccup.
Lough	vaguely like the Scottish *loch*.

I'm not totally convinced by the spelling of hough (*hoof*), although that would make ten different pronunciations, I believe, which is surely a world record.

As we've already seen, the vagaries of English spelling are partly because English has had to cope with words that have come in from dozens of different languages. This way, we have the -F sound in *football*, because F is a good, Germanic letter. Then we go and get something from Greek, such as *photograph*, where we've got completely different spellings, and use the *ph* combination to arrive at the sound.

It's also partly because we've got around 44 different sounds (technically called phonemes – oh, there's that -F sound again), but only 26 letters to do the job. There used to be a letter called the thorn, which when hand-written resembled the modern Y that had the *th* sound. It still lives on today in *Ye Olde Tea-Shoppe*. *Ye* would have been pronounced *the*. Shame we've lost that – it would have been a useful letter to have kept.

Not only is it hard to anticipate how to spell something when we hear the word, but when we see it written down, we don't always know how to pronounce it either. Take a couple of examples.

| *Bow* | Pronounce it one way and it means a greeting by bending from the waist. Pronounce it another way and you've got something Robin Hood carried around |

	along with his arrows or a loop of string or ribbon.
Desert	Were you thinking of the Sahara or running away from the army?
Refuse	Was it rubbish, or didn't you want it?
Lead	Was it a metal or something to attach to a dog's collar?

We also have what they call homophones, such as *steak/stake, mane/main, right/write/rite, new/knew* or *their, they're* and *there.*

The notion of standard spelling is a modern idea. Shakespeare didn't bother too much. He spelled his own name four different ways, not including abbreviated forms. It was only when the first printing presses started turning that there was any real thought about some kind of standardisation of spelling. To begin with, it would simply be individual printers, who were often publishers and booksellers as well, who decided how they were going to spell any given word. With the advent of the first real dictionaries, such as Dr. Johnson's *Dictionary of the English Language* in 1755 and Noah Webster's *A Compendious Dictionary of the English Language*, published half a century later in America, spelling began to become increasingly standardised.

The idea of 'correct' spelling is thus relatively recent. The advantage of standard spelling is that anyone who understands English, no matter what their local accent, can follow the written word. One person may use the short *a* to say the word *bath*, which is typical of the northern half of the UK, but another may pronounce it with the long *a*, so that its sounds like *baaath* (or even *baaarf*). But when northerners or southerners see it written down, they know what it means.

From the 16th Century right through to the 1960s, there have been attempts to make the system more logical. Amongst advocates of reform were Mark Twain in America and George Bernard Shaw in the UK. Even Lord Baden-Powell took time out from looking after boys in shorts to advocate reform. And earlier still, Benjamin Franklin decided that there weren't enough letters to do the job properly, so he invented several, including new ones for the *ch* and *-ng* sounds.

Obviously, these changes never caught on. But people are inventive at coming up with their own spellings. There is currently a great deal of debate as to whether or not textspeak (*txtspk*) is damaging the nation's children and turning them into semi-literate hoodlums (or should that be hoodla?).

The myth has it that when forced to write in real sentences, these kids are reduced to writing *ATM* (*at the moment*) or *LOL* (*laugh out loud*) or *CUL8R* (*see you later*). The noted writer on matters of language and grammar, David Crystal, has derided this. Besides, you only need to think for a moment to realise that we've always done this. *Geo. Smith Ltd.* is short for *George Smith, Limited*. The aforementioned William Shakespeare signed at least one document as *Wm Shakesp.*

Wherever we have written language, we have ways of abbreviating it, of finding our own shorthand. Aren't *1,2,3,4* a kind of quick way of writing *one, two, three, four*? Most of us are bright enough to work out that we can use txtspk for our texts and full sentences with beautifully honed grammar and spelling for our school essays. A text message sent to a friend is allowed misspellings, matey language or quirky usage. On the other hand, they might just be a deal-breaker when trying to broker a multi-million pound contract.

As we move into the part of this book dedicated to helping you 'get things right', remember that we're all fallible. The 'rules' aren't precisely rules, and that they change all the time. Conventions that I learned at school just a generation ago no longer hold sway. I'm continually perplexed by hyphenated words. When did *girl-friend* suddenly become *girlfriend*? Above all, don't be intimidated. It's not your fault if your English teacher short-changed you.

6

Some Hoary Old Grammatical Chestnuts

Before we get into the nuts and bolts of grammar, let's take a gander at some common mistakes. Several of these get real grammarians boiling hot under the collar. True, sometimes, you wonder why anyone should care, especially when the meaning of what is written is obvious or they're applying 'rules' from another language that are irrelevant to English. However, incorrect grammar is like a hole in a leaky boat. Readers lose faith in someone who keeps on making mistakes.

Quite unique/very unique/absolutely unique

If something is *unique,* it is one of a kind.

The word derives from the Latin for *one.* Therefore, if it's *unique,* you can't have varying degrees of uniqueness. *Quite unique?* It's like being a *little bit pregnant.*

Amount/Number, Less/Fewer

A confession – I'm a bit old-fashioned on this one. I actively dislike it when I hear BBC reporters saying, 'The amount of people here at Wimbledon today is astonishing'. It really should be, 'The *number* of people is astonishing.'

In theory, you should use *number* and *fewer* for anything you can count. As we could have counted the number of people at Wimbledon, then we should use the word *number*. *Amount* is for something uncountable. We could talk about the *amount* of beer brewed in the world or the *amount* of money in circulation in the economy.

Similarly, when the same reporter then announces, 'There are less people here today at Wimbledon than there were yesterday', she's also getting it wrong. Less is also uncountable. There are *fewer* people.

One of the reasons for getting this right is that you then don't have old duffers like me getting out the green ink to write in to complain.

Quote/Quotation, Invite/Invitation

Strictly speaking *quote* and *invite* are verbs. In theory, your essay contains *quotations*, not *quotes*, and your *invitation* is not an *invite*. It's best to avoid using *quotes* and *invites* as nouns in formal writing.

That/Which

I once read Julian Barnes on the subject of the correct use of that and which but can't for the life of me find the essay in which he did so. If I remember rightly, he said essentially that he alternated them so as not to appear as though he was repeating the same word too often, which got his American editor slightly wound up.

Now if Julian Barnes, Chevalier of the Legion d'Honneur, and winner of the Man Booker prize, isn't entirely sure how to use these two, then I'm not sure why the rest of us should worry. But some people do.

First of all, you can't use *that* for people as it is bad grammar:

*The man **that** she got engaged to is standing over there.*

It should be:

*The man **to whom** she got engaged ...*

Even if that does sound a bit pompous. However, *that* is fine for:

*This is the house **that** I am hoping to buy ...*

Or it should be:

*This is the house **which** I am hoping to buy?*

Well, British English probably allows you to use either when referring to important information. In the above example, the important information is that we're identifying the precise house – it's the one I'm going to buy. There doesn't seem to be a hard and fast rule to this. But, in the following cases, where the additional information isn't crucial to the grammar of the sentence, then you need to use *which*:

*We stood outside the house, **which** was the one I intended to buy, and gazed up at its mullioned windows.*

*His car, **which** happened to be parked in the street, was daubed with angry graffiti.*

In these cases, it's the *mullioned windows* and the *graffiti* which are at the heart of the sentence, so the extra information can be introduced with *which*.

The Split Infinitive

The most famous split infinitive of all time is on the voice-over for the original Star Trek series:

*To **boldly** go where no man has gone before.*

The infinitive *to go* is split by having the word *boldly* shoved into it. Now, the difficulty with this idea is that there is arguably no such thing as the infinitive in English. *Go* is a stem word onto which we add various endings to make new variants — *gone* or *going* or *goes*. The term infinitive exists so that we can have a direct translation for some foreign words — traditionally words from Latin. So, the Latin *amare* means *to love*. In the Latin language, you can't actually split the word *amare*, it has to stay as one word. This then got brought into English as a 'rule'.

Of course, you can split the infinitive if you want to. After all Captain James Tiberius Kirk has been doing it regularly for decades. However, it's one of those phrases that has some people sucking their teeth like a plumber about to quote for new pipework.

Despite the fact that the idea of the split infinitive was the concoction of some loopy 18th Century bishop, the rule seems to have grammarians tut-tutting to this day. Brought up on it myself, I find it hard to break. That's ridiculous. Break the rule by all means but do be wary if the result is convoluted and ugly, especially when you split the infinitive with an adverbial phrase.

*The company is hoping to **in the long-term** increase employees' salaries*

can be re-arranged to:

The company is hoping to increase employees' salaries in the long term.

It's also easier to understand.

Ending a Sentence with a Preposition

For some reason, it was also decreed by the great and the good that you shouldn't end a sentence with a preposition. Prepositions are words such as *to, with, from, by, for*, etc.

In theory, if you write:

*This is the town they're travelling **to**.*

You should re-arrange it to read:

*This is the town **to** which they are travelling.*

Frankly, this does seem petty, especially as neither sentence in the example above is good, plain English (*They are travelling to this town*). It's fine if you want to disentangle a mess, like that deliberately written by the humourist H.L. Mencken, 'Why did you bring that book that I didn't want to be read to out of up for?'

Even Winston Churchill famously condemned pedantry over the no-preposition-at-the-end rule when some young editor had fiddled with his prose by saying something along the lines of:

This is the sort of language up with which I will not put.

Don't forget Churchill was a journalist by training and he also went on to win the Nobel Prize for Literature. Shakespeare too was happy to write, '*We are the stuff as dreams are made on*.' There are some high-ranking precedents for ignoring this 'rule'.

On the other hand, the Hemingway novel is not called *Who the Bell Tolls for*.

Double Negative

You'll hear this much more than you'll ever read it. In mathematics, if you multiply two negative numbers, you get a positive result (-2 x -3 = 6). Somehow, this idea migrated into grammar, where if you say:

I'm not never going there again

Some people argue that this means that you definitely are going there again as the two negatives cancel each other out. In reality, that's linguistic snobbery. The person saying this really isn't going to visit this place again. That's obvious. Besides, usually when people come to write, they don't use their exact spoken grammar, so this doesn't become a problem. Written down, a double negative just looks like bad English. A simple *I'm **never** going there again* would suffice.

He Was Sat/He Was Sitting and She Was Stood/She Was Standing

When we speak, we often say things such as:

*He was **sat** in the corner, drinking a pint.*

It's fine in speech, but possibly slightly poor in terms of formal grammar. Assuming that he actually sat himself down to drink his beer, we should more correctly write:

*He was **sitting** in the corner, drinking a pint.*

This isn't necessarily being pedantic. There is a precise difference in meaning between these two sentences. He *was sat* means that someone actually positioned him there. He *was sitting* (or *was seated*) implies he's managed to park his rear all by himself.

The guards were stood by the door.
The guards had been positioned by the door.

She was standing by the door.
She'd gone and put herself in an upright position by the door.

Who/Whom

We've talked about the concept of inflection elsewhere: the idea that some words change according to their grammatical function, the most obvious inflection being adding *s* to most nouns to indicate that we're in the plural (e.g. *cow/cows, glove/ gloves*).

Who is used for the subject of sentences, i.e., for the person doing the action? *Whom* is used when *who* becomes the object of a sentence.

> **Who** *is that masked man?* (*Who* is the subject)
> *For* **whom** *is that mask? Might it be Zorro?* (*Whom* is the object)
> *To* **whom** *it may concern.*
> *For* **whom** *the bell tolls.*

You can get a tad precious over *who* and *whom*. As Clarence Darrow once wrote, 'Even if you learn to speak correct English, to whom are you going to speak it?'

If you're uncertain, use *who*. For some reason, it's worse using *whom* wrongly, than it is messing up *who*.

I/Me/Myself

I is for the subject of a sentence. *Me* is for the object of a sentence. *Myself* is for reflexive use, such as things you do to yourself:

> **I** *ate an entire block of chocolate.*
> *The policeman gave* **me** *a dirty look.*
> *I'm going to sit right down and write* **myself** *a letter.*
> *I will do that* **myself***.*

Where people tend to get confused is when they think they are using the word *I* too much. To get round this, they think that *me* or *myself* might sound better, perhaps less egotistical. They then start substituting *me* or *myself* for *I*.

Helen and **myself** *are working on this case.*

This is wrong. It should simply be:

Helen and **I** *are working on this case.*

Older/Oldest, Younger/Youngest, Bigger/Biggest, etc.

(See also under Adjectives in the Parts of Speech section)

The basic adjectives at the roots of these words are *old, young* and *big*. We use *bigger, younger, older* when we are comparing two items or people. This form of the adjective is called the comparative.

The form of the adjective that means the most big (*biggest*), the most young (*youngest*), the most old (*oldest*) is called the superlative. You need at least three items or people to be able to use the superlative. If there are just two, then you can only use the comparative.

There are two boys in his family and Paul is the **older***. Melanie is the* **oldest** *of three children.*

This is the **biggest** *audience we've ever had. We had a* **bigger** *audience this week than we did last week.*

Awkward Singulars and Plurals

Normally deciding whether a verb should be singular or plural is easy.

The boy **is** *standing on the burning deck.*
Singular, so we have *is*.

The boys **are** *standing on the burning deck.*
Plural, so we use *are*.

The difficulty seems to be when we start talking about groups of people, especially sports teams and businesses. Strictly speaking if we write:

*England **are** going to win the Jules Rimet Trophy*

not only are we being vaguely delusional, but we are pairing up *England* (singular) with the verb *are* (plural). Technically, we are incorrect. In fact, it's one of the big bugbears of American English-grammar-tub-thumpers. They want us to write:

*England **is** going to win the Jules Rimet Trophy.*

I think it's being a bit pernickety and would suggest that the following uses are fine:

*Liverpool **are** playing well this season.*

We're referring to the men who make up the team. (As I write, they are playing well, but in the first edition of this book, it was an outright lie.)

*Liverpool **is** a club with a long tradition.*

Technically, this is better grammar, although we could still get away with a singular noun and a plural verb.

*Liverpool **are** a great club.*

If we're referring to the place as a whole, we would write:

*Liverpool **is** a great city.*

What else could you use but a singular verb? *Liverpool **are** a great city* would sound ridiculous. Similarly:

*Scotland **are** in the finals. Scotland **is** a beautiful country.*

Beware! There are some plural words that do get misused in the singular:

*The main **criteria** for buying this house is its location.*

This is wrong. The word *criteria* is already plural. The singular of *criteria* is *criterion*. So, you should write:

The main criterion for buying this house is its location.

Don't forget that the word *none* is usually singular. *None of us are perfect* is technically incorrect. *None of us is perfect.* However, this is nit-picking in the extreme. Similarly, if you use a construction with *neither of*, you also have to use a singular verb. *Neither of them is perfect.*

Compare to/Compare with

*Shall I compare thee **to** a summer's day?*

To what extent are you like a summer's day? You're not comparing like with like. You're comparing a person to a day in a particular season; something completely different.

*Compared **with** Juliet, Rosalind is a little scatty.*

Here, you're comparing within the same category — two Shakespearean heroines. So, you're comparing one *with* another. This distinction does seem to be disappearing and it may be a bit pedantic to include it, but there we go.

Dangling Participles (Hanging Participles)

This is where we accidentally cement two halves of a sentence that don't fit with each other.

Learning to play golf, the putting was the easiest part.

Who's learning to play golf? The putting? Obviously not. This just needs disentangling:

When I was learning to play golf, putting was the easiest part.

Similarly, in a sentence such as this:

Travelling to work, the pillar-box was vandalised...

... the implication is that the pillar-box is doing the travelling, which is unlikely.

As he was travelling to work, he noticed that the pillar-box was vandalised.

Like/As/As if/Such as

Read these sentences and think which of them may be correct:

1. *He ran like a gazelle does.*
2. *He ran like a gazelle.*
3. *He ran as a gazelle.*
4. *He ran as a gazelle does.*

Full marks if you opted for sentences 2 and 4, although 4 sounds dreadfully stilted or as if it then wants some kind of qualifying statement.

*He ran **as** a gazelle does: on all fours and with nostrils flaring.*

In a nutshell, *like* is a preposition. It can't come in front of a complete clause that contains a finite verb. On the other hand, *as* is a conjunction — it can join two halves of a sentence/two clauses. So:

*We were able to get to London **as** the motorway was clear.*
***As** you've got a day off, you can clear the garage out.*

Like can also be used to start a list:

*He ate tinned food, **like** spaghetti hoops and baked beans.*

But, it has too much of an informal ring about it for most forms of writing. You're better using *such as* instead:

*He ate tinned food, **such as** spaghetti hoops and baked beans.*
*In those days we played games, **such as** tag, British Bulldog and knockdown ginger.*
*The menu includes several fish dishes, **such as** salmon, trout, haddock and plaice.*

Or in this context:

*He looked **like** he could do with a good holiday in the sun.*

This is probably a bit too informal when written down, so use *as if* instead:

*He looked **as if** he could do with a good holiday in the sun.*
*It looks **as if** the weather might improve over the next few days.*

If/Whether

On some occasions, you can use *whether* or *if* interchangeably.

*I'm not sure **whether** she's coming with us or staying at home.*
*I'm not sure **if** she's coming with us or staying at home.*

However, *whether* does often carry with it the idea of choice. The following sentence simply doesn't sound right:

*She asked me **whether** I'd be happier sitting in the shade.*

We'd be better off using *if*:

*She asked me **if** I'd be happier sitting in the shade.*

Or, if we insist on using *whether*:

*She asked me **whether** I'd be happier sitting in the shade or in direct sunlight.*

You can't use *if* before an infinitive (to + verb).

I don't know if to sit in the sun or not.

This is obviously wrong, so use *whether*:

*I don't know **whether** to sit in the sun or not.*

As with anything, reading a sentence out loud will soon show you what sounds right.

Awkward Plurals

There's the famous gag about the man who wants to mail-order two little mammals to keep as pets. He starts off his letter:

Dear Sir, please send me two mongooses.
He doesn't like the sound of that, so he starts again:

Dear Sir, please send me two mongeese.
He's not happy with that either, so he writes:

Dear Sir, please send me two mongeeses.
No, that's even worse. Clever chap, he pens:

Dear Sir, please send me a mongoose. PS, please send me another one.

Do you know which is correct?

Forming plurals in English is normally straightforward. More often than not, you just add *-s*.

Computer	*computers*
Monkey	*monkeys*

Some nouns need *-es* to form the plural. These tend to be nouns ending in -ch, or -sh.

Church	*churches*
Bitch	*bitches*

| *Radish* | *radishes* |
| *Polish* | *polishes* |

Nouns ending in consonant *-y* take *-ies* for the plural

Cherry	*cherries*
Belly	*bellies*
Sky	*skies*

Although if they end in vowel -y, they don't:

Monkey	*monkeys*
Donkey	*donkeys*
Days	*days*

Words Ending in -O

Words ending in *-o* tend to be tricky. Various people have tried to provide useful guides as to when just to add an *-s* and when you need *-es*. Sometimes, it's personal references, for instance you can pluralise *volcano* to both *volcanos* and *volcanoes*. However, there are other words such as *buffalo, hero* and *mosquito* that have to take *-es*, yet more simply take *-s*, such as *zero, solo, studio, video*.

What they definitely do not do is take apostrophe-s, despite the fact that you see *video's* written everywhere. Added to the trickiness is the fact that there are some Italian words ending in *-o*, such as *paparazzo*, which take *-i* in the plural — *paparazzi*.

A Rule-of-thumb for Latin and Greek Plurals

In some cases, we have leftovers from Latin and Greek or more modern foreign imports and they can be a bit tricky.

Words ending in *-a* become *-ae*	*alumna, alumnae*
Words ending in *-um* become *-a*	*aquarium, aquaria* (this form of pluralisation is falling out of fashion, so we have *aquariums*)
Words ending in *-us* become *-i*	*alumnus, alumni*
Words ending in *-ex* become *-ices*	*codex, codices*
Words ending in *-on* become *-a*	*criterion, criteria*
Words ending in *-is* become *-es*	*neurosis, neuroses*

So how do you know if they're Latin or Greek? You can't tell, but if they look Latin or Greek, chances are ...

Here's a handful of awkward plurals to keep you busy:

Agenda	It's already plural, the singular is *agendum*. That sounds pretentious, so you're probably better off referring to an *agenda item*.
Appendix	*Appendixes* if referring to a part of the body, *appendices* for matter at the end of a book.
Au Pair	It should be *aux pairs* but tends to be *au pairs*. In French, you have to make adjectives, nouns and articles agree.
Automaton	*Automata*. (Like *criterion-criteria*.)
Beau	*Beaux*. If you have more than one gentleman caller, then you have several *beaux*.
Bus	*Buses*. If you double the *-s* to get *busses*, you're then referring to quick kisses.
Calf	*Calves*. As with *wolf, wife, loaf* and *half*.
Château Châteaux	(from the French. It's also *gâteau/gâteaux*, although *bureaux* and *bureaus* are both acceptable for *bureau*).

Child	*Children.*
Court Martial	*Courts Martial.* It's the courts that are plural, not the fact that they're martial i.e., pertaining to the military.
Crocus	*Crocuses* (apparently, it's not Latin, so *croci* is wrong).
Data	This is already plural, based on the Latin word *datum*. It should, therefore, take a plural verb, e.g. *The data **show** us that this is the case.* It sounds odd when you say it aloud, but if you're writing formal documents, then it's best to get it right.
Dwarf	*Dwarfs.* Not *dwarves*, as many people think, although my (non-tabloid) newspaper is happy to use it and some sources state that both are correct.
Fish	*Fish or fishes* (but doesn't *fishes* sound a little childish?).
Foot	*Feet* (although when measuring people or things, you can get away with the singular: *five foot two, eyes of blue*).
Formula	Technically, it should be *formulae*, but *formulas* is fine. Perhaps it's best to use *formulae* in mathematics/science, but *formulas* for other use.
Gallows	It's either singular or plural anyway.
Goose	*Geese.* Ah, but it's *mongooses*. So now you know.
Medium	*Media*, if we're referring to TV, newspapers etc. *Mediums*, if we mean spiritualists with wine glasses and tarot cards on green-baized tables.

Mouse	*Mice,* although for some reason, this never sounds right when you're dealing with computer equipment. However, it is exactly the same for rodents as it is for inputting devices.
Opera	*Operas.* In theory, opera is already the plural form of *opus,* but it's now established as a singular word in English.
Panini	It's already plural, the singular is *panino.* It's Italian, as are words such as *graffiti* (*graffito*), *paparazzi* (*paparazzo*). In theory, you should probably order two *cappuccini* rather than two *cappuccinos.* You just have to accept that *panini* has now entered English as a singular noun.
Phobia	*Phobias.*
Sheep	*Sheep.*
Stadium	*Stadiums* or *stadia.* Both seem to be in use. *Stadia* sounds a little pretentious, but I've seen it on road signs.
Tomato	*Tomatoes.* And *potato* becomes *potatoes.*
Tooth	*Teeth.*
Virtuoso	*Virtuosi* looks a bit ostentatious, so perhaps best to stick with *virtuosos.*

8

Confusable words

There are so many English words that are easy to confuse that there are several fat books devoted to the subject. What follows is a choice selection of some of the most common linguistic trip hazards. Some of these are obvious, but often occur as typos (it's easy to type *to* for *too*) and aren't picked up by spell-checkers. Others are trickier and some defy logic completely.

Abuse/Misuse

Both are concerned with doing bad deeds. *Abuse* is stronger than *misuse*. If you *abuse* a child, you are doing them genuine damage. In tennis matches, you can be docked points for *racquet abuse*. This generally means smashing up your racquet or hurling it at an innocent spectator or line judge. *Misuse* of a tennis racket is what Jack Lemmon does in the film 'The Apartment', when he uses one to strain spaghetti. Using a spaghetti strainer to play tennis would also be a form of *misuse*: a tennis racquet is not designed to strain spaghetti and a spaghetti strainer is not designed for tennis.

Adverse/Averse

Adverse tends to mean difficult, unfavourable, possibly even hostile. It crops up in phrases such as *adverse trading conditions*, when we mean that the economy is having a tough time. *Adverse publicity* and *adverse weather conditions* are two other common uses. If you are *averse* to something, it means you don't like it. You may be *averse* to housework, which means your carpets are gritty and your shelves dusty. Occasionally, you might hear someone say something along the lines of, 'I'm not averse to a bit of pork pie.' It works better spoken than it ever does in print. Usually, you cannot use the word *adverse* when referring to people, whereas *averse* almost always refers to a person.

Advice/Advise

Advice is the noun, *advise* the verb. Try saying them aloud and you'll see hear the difference. When you give someone *advice*, you are *advising* them.

Affect/Effect

This is a particularly tricky one. Generally, *affect* is the verb and *effect* is the noun, but ...you can use *affect* as a noun, but it tends to have a specific meaning in the field of psychology. For instance, psychopaths display shallow *affect*, which means that don't have the same depth of feelings as normal people. However, for most ordinary use, *affect* will be a verb. Typical uses of *affect* would be:

*Alcohol **affects** your ability to drive.* In other words, it has an influence on the way you drive. Often the influence implied by the word is a negative one.

*After he had smashed the window, Burglar Bill **affected** an air of nonchalance.* He pretended to be nonchalant.

You can also use it as a verb to mean 'emotionally move'. *I watched his performance of King Lear and was genuinely **affected** by it.* This use seems to be getting rarer.

In theory, you can use the word *effect* as a verb:

*The company has **effected** a wage-freeze policy.* Here *effect* means to bring about or to implement. It's an ugly usage, as you'll probably agree.

In the main, think of *effect* as a noun:

*I'd like to think that our fiscal policy has some **effect** on the economy.* *Effect* = influence.

*The **effect** of our fiscal policy is that the economy is in tatters.* *Effect* = result.

*We need to put this fiscal plan into **effect** immediately.* *Put into effect* is a set phrase, meaning put into place or put into operation.

Allowed/Aloud

Allowed means *permitted*; *aloud* means *out loud*. Think *loud noise* and it helps you get to the spelling of *aloud*.

All right/Alright

Technically, in British English, you should use *all right*. However, *alright* is now in common usage. Some older people might take offence, but then they like a moan. Just buy them a packet of their favourite boiled sweets and let them get on with it.

Allusion/Illusion

An *allusion* is something you refer to. If we say that we're in a *Catch-22 situation*, this is an *allusion* to the book by Joseph Heller. An *illusion* is something you imagine seeing. Sawing a lady in half is an *illusion*. Well it is usually.

Alternate/Alternative

Alternate, when used as a verb, means something along the lines of *change between/switch between*: *She has bi-polar disorder. Her mood **alternates** between intense depression and hyperactivity.*

As an adjective *alternate* means happening by turns. If you go to the cinema on *alternate* Saturdays, one week you go to see a film, the next you don't.

Alternative normally contains the idea of choice. *You can have either beef and all the trimmings, or the vegetarian* **alternative**. *Alternative* can also nowadays mean something that is not in the mainstream or is unconventional. The term *alternative comedy* was coined to refer to jokes that weren't about fat people, mothers-in-law, and Irish labourers. *Alternative medicine* refers to treatments where there is no scientific proof of their effectiveness. Be wary of tautology. *There is* **another alternative** *we can investigate.* Here, you're saying the same thing twice. An *alternative* is *another*.

Amend/Emend

There's so little difference between these two that it's hard to differentiate. Both words carry the meaning of changing something. If you read through what you have written and then *amend* it, you are *making it better*. The implication is that you're changing sentences round, cutting words (or whatever) to improve what you've written. On the other hand, if you *emend*, you just correct typos and such. Parliament *amends* laws, for instance, but a proofreader looks for *emendations*. If in doubt, avoid the word *emend*. *Amend* will serve for most purposes.

Amiable/Amicable

Both words have the same idea — that of being friendly, from the French verb *aimer*. *Amiable* is used when we're talking about people. *He's an amiable chap*. *Amicable* is most often used in set phrases such as *amicable divorce settlement, amicable agreement, amicable conversation* or *amicable relationship*.

Appraise/Apprise

Appraise is concerned with making judgements about someone or something. It's approximately the equivalent of *assess* or *evaluate*. *Once we can get into the flooded building, we can* **appraise** *the amount of damage.* If you think of the noun form, *appraisal*, which is most commonly used for a yearly pantomime when your boss tells you how your work is going, then it's easy to remember the difference. *Apprise* means to inform. *We* **apprised** *him of the situation* = We told him what was happening.

Assume/Presume

It's no wonder people have trouble with these two as their meanings do tend to overlap. If you *assume* something, you suppose something without evidence or proof. Some people *assume* that their star sign will influence the way they behave, but there is no scientific evidence to support this thinking. *Presume* is to expect something without having any reason why we should think otherwise. If you always meet your mate at the pub on a Sunday, you might write: *I* **presumed** *he would be at the Fool and Bladder on Sunday, so I was surprised when he didn't turn up.* It wasn't an unreasonable notion that he would be in the pub, given he'd been there the previous 50-odd weeks. *Presume* also carries an additional meaning — that of being a little bit forward, perhaps taking things a step too far. You'll come across this most often in the adjective *presumptuous*. *She helped herself to my finest single malt whisky, which was a bit* **presumptuous**.

Assurance/Insurance

In the *insurance* industry, which is concerned with covering risks, we have *household insurance, motor insurance, contents insurance* and so on. For some reason insuring a person's life is called *life assurance*. Why this difference exists is beyond me.

With luck, things will change and all we'll have is the word *insurance*. Apart from that single use of *life assurance, assurance* is concerned with giving someone a guarantee or a certainty. *You have my **assurance** that the job will be finished by Thursday.* I *promise* the job will be done by then.

Assure/Insure/Ensure

Assure = guarantee, convince
Insure = offset risk, guarantee against loss
Ensure = to make something certain

*We **assured** the customer we could do the job by Thursday. We brought in an extra pair of hands to **ensure** that we had the job done in time. Meanwhile, the manager **insured** the building against fire, flood and bubonic plague.*

Aural/Oral

Nasty this, because they're normally pronounced the same way. Both have Latin roots. *Aural* is to do with the ear; *oral* is the mouth. You have to make a little round O-shape with your mouth to make the sound *oral*, so that may be one way of remembering it. If you can't, then look for alternatives. An *aural* examination is a listening test; an *oral* test denotes speaking.

Bare/Bear

Bare means *naked*. *Bear* is used for the *furry animal*, the *right to* ***bear** arms* and pretty much anything else.

Blatant/Flagrant

Both words tend to mean the same thing and are probably soon going to be interchangeable, but *flagrant* is stronger than *blatant*. In football, you often get *blatant* fouls. These are deliberate, often minor, infringements of the rules, such as barging a man off the ball. Occasionally, you will get a foul so nasty that it may be re-categorised as *flagrant*. If the goal-keeper races to the half-way line and rugby-tackles the opposing forward, breaking the poor man's ribs in the process, then jumps up and down on his prostrate form, then that is a *flagrant* foul. *Blatant* is obvious, but *flagrant* contains the notion of something scandalous. Stealing a couple of ball-point pens from your place of work is *blatantly* wrong. Diverting the entire company's income for the last three years into your personal bank account is a *flagrant* breech of the rules.

Brake/Break

Brake normally has the meaning of *stopping* or *slowing down*, so a car has *brakes*. *Break* is for pretty much every other use — *smash, interval between work sessions, deciphering codes, waves on the beach...*

Cannon/Canon

Cannon is used when we're writing about artillery or snooker and billiards. *Canon* is a musical term; you may well know *Pachelbel's Canon in D Major* (or you'd probably recognise it if you heard it). There are also *canons* in the clergy: it's a rank in several different churches. We also sometimes refer to the *literary canon*, or the *artistic canon*. Essentially, this means works of literature (or art) that have come to be regarded as classics.

Canvas/Canvass

Canvas is what tents and sails used to be made of back in the pre-decimal dark ages. It's a heavy-duty material. If you *canvass* someone, then you're asking for their opinion. The meaning has also broadened out to include the concept of electioneering. *The*

Conservative candidate for Smelling-in-the-Pit, Peregrine Oldetonian, was out **canvassing** *earlier today.* In other words, he was trying to drum up some votes.

Check/Cheque

In British English, a *cheque* is a piece of signed paper stating that you owe someone a certain amount of money, hence *cheque book*. Older readers will recall these. *Check* is used for all other meanings (and indeed is also the US spelling of the word *cheque*).

Cereal/Serial

Cereals are crops and what you eat for breakfast. A *serial* is something that is presented in instalments, e.g., a *television serial* is a programme that develops on an episode-by-episode basis.

Chute/Shoot

A *chute* is normally a kind of slide, such as a *laundry chute*. It can be used to mean a *cascade of water* too. All other meanings of the word pronounced like this, such as *make an attempt on goal, fire a gun, move quickly*, etc. need the spelling *shoot*.

Cite/Sight/Site

Cite is usually another word for *quote*, in the sense of referring to what someone has said or written, although the word *quote* probably carries with it the idea that you get the information verbatim. You can't use *cite* in the sense of *giving an estimation*. *He asked me what I thought it would cost and I* **quoted** *him a thousand pounds.*

Sight is the noun associated with the verb *see*. The *sights* of Paris would include the Eiffel Tower, the Arc de Triomphe and the Sacré-Coeur, for instance. If you connect it to the word *eyesight*, it's easier to remember.

Site is another word for location. You'll come across it in phrases such as *building site* or *site of the accident*. It comes from the same root as the word *situation*.

Climatic/Climactic

Climatic is to do with climate and weather. *Climactic* is when something comes to a head, to a climax. If you go back to the nouns they come from (*climate/climax*), it's easier to remember which is which.

Compliment/Complement (Complimentary/Complementary)

A *compliment* is a positive statement. *Give your wife my* **compliments** means to send her good wishes. *Complimentary* can also mean free-of-charge. *They gave us* **complimentary** *tickets to the cinema. Complement* literally means something that fills something up, it comes from the same root as *complete*. We get it in phrases such as *a full complement of drivers*, in other words, we have enough drivers for the fleet of vehicles. If you see a sign advertising *Complimentary Medicine*, they've spelled it wrong. Go up to the assistant and ask him or her to say nice things to you. *Complement* is also a grammatical term. In a sentence such as *She was an astronaut, she* is the subject, but *an astronaut* is not the object (it doesn't have anything done to it, it's a noun describing her), so *an astronaut* is a *complement* — the idea is that *an astronaut* completes the sentence.

Confidant(e)/Confident

A *confidant*, or if a woman, a *confidante*, is somebody you would *confide* in, someone to whom you'd tell secrets (and expect them to keep them). *Confident* is an adjective meaning more-or-less the opposite of nervous.

Continual/Continuous

Continual refers to something that continues but has interruptions. A tap drips *continually*. *Continuous* refers to something that continues without interruptions, such as the *continuous* gurgling of a stream or when you turn the tap on properly.

Credible/Credulous

Something that is *credible* is believable. It is *credible* that there might be life elsewhere in the galaxy. Although you can apply the word credible to people, it tends to be in specific phrases, such as *she made a **credible** witness*. The jury was likely to believe her. *Credulous* is applied only to people. It means approximately the same as *gullible*.

Years ago, I was lucky enough to be able to play this old trick, first used by Socrates in 430 BCE, on an A-level General Studies group. We came across the word *credulous* in whatever it was we were studying and one of them asked what the word meant. I grabbed the dictionary from the desk drawer and looked through it. 'It's not in here. That's appalling. I can't believe it's not in my dictionary.' The student duly trotted off to the library, came back with another, bigger dictionary and read out the definition. Oh, how we laughed when it dawned on her what a cunning, ironic trick I had pulled. We all learnt a lesson that day. They learned about public humiliation, and I now know how to protect my head and face when attacked by an 18-year-old wielding a heavy dictionary.

Criterion/criteria

Criterion is the singular and *criteria* plural. A *criterion* is an accepted standard or principle for making judgments and decisions.

Currant/Current

A *currant* is a type of dried fruit that you often find in buns. *Current* refers to electricity, moving water, being up-to-date or anything else other than dried fruit.

Definite/Definitive

You'll see these confused most often in the phrases **definite** *answer* and **definitive** *answer*. A **definite** *answer* is an exact answer (*We now know we can install the computer system on Thursday*); a **definitive** *answer* is unchallengeable — it comes from the best authority, so scientists might provide a **definitive** *answer* as to why cancer cells grow.

Defuse/Diffuse

Defuse literally means to take the fuse out of something (*de-fuse*). You *defuse* a bomb, from which comes the phrase *defuse a situation*. *Diffuse* is concerned with scattering or spreading out. One of its most common uses is to describe a kind of scattered light that doesn't glare: *diffused* light.

Dependant/Dependent

A *dependant* must be a person. If you're the breadwinner for the family, you have *dependants*. They rely on you for support. *Dependent* is the adjective. Your *dependants* are *dependent* on you. You'll also come across the word in phrases such as **dependent** *on the results*, **dependent** *on their agreement*. You can often substitute the word *depending* in these cases, which gives you a clue to spelling, or if you're not sure, just use *depending*.

Deprecate/Depreciate

Although there is technically an overlap between these two words, that is now disappearing. If you *deprecate* something, you disapprove of it strongly. *He **deprecates** violence. Depreciate* means to go down in value. *My shares have **depreciated** badly over the last year.* In other words, they are not worth what I paid for them.

Disc/Disk

Strictly speaking, anything that is circular, such as a record or a plate is a *disc*. *Disk* is the American spelling and it came into use with computers, which needed *floppy disks* and *hard disks* to store information. *Disk* therefore tends to be used in computing terminology, *disc* for anything else, including *compact discs*.

Discreet/Discrete

Someone who is *discreet* shows some kind of reserve or tact. It is often used about a person you could rely on to keep a confidence or a secret. It is related to the word *discretion*. *Discrete* means separate.

Disinterested/Uninterested

Disinterested means *impartial*. In football matches, they have a referee, who should be *disinterested*. In other words, s/he should not have an interest in either side. If you are *uninterested*, it means you don't care. You may be *uninterested* in football, so you switch off the TV when it comes on. However, as most people don't know the difference, it's not a bad idea to stop using the word *disinterested* altogether. If you use *disinterested* in its precise meaning, too many people are going to think you meant that you *couldn't care*, so what's the point in hacking them off by mistake?

Distinct/Distinctive

Distinct means something along the lines of *clear, obvious* or *likely. There was a **distinct** possibility of rain. Distinctive* is related to something being different and probably having an unmistakable characteristic. We refer to a *distinctive flavour* or a *distinctive smell.* A zebra has *distinctive markings.*

Draft/Draught

A *draft* is generally something on paper. It's often a sketch or a version of a piece of writing or can mean *a cheque.* It can also mean *a detachment of troops*, although this is not used often. In the USA, the *draft* refers to a system of compulsory military service. *Draught* refers to pulling things (*draughthorse*), drinks (including *draught beer*) or a current of air. In the plural (*draughts*) it is used for the game played on a chessboard (checkers if you prefer).

Draw/Drawer

Draw has the meaning of making a picture. *Draw* also means to pull, as in the phrase horse-*drawn* carriage. The confusion mainly arrives when we're referring to the box that slides in and out of a cabinet, desk or a table. It is a *drawer,* as in *chest of drawers.*

Elder/Older

These can be used interchangeably when the word means *more old. John and Peter are brothers. John is the **older**. John is the **elder**.* On its own, the word *elder* can refer to people who have the gravitas of age and seniority, as in the *Elders of the Tribe* or *Elders of the Church. Elder* is also a kind of shrub that produces berries and flowers.

Emigrate/Immigrate (Emigrant/Immigrant)

Someone who *emigrates* leaves their own country. If I leave the lovely English weather to go and shiver in the South of France, I am *emigrating*. To the French, though, I will be an *immigrant* as from their point-of-view, I have *immigrated.*

Emotional/Emotive

An *emotional* speech would probably display the emotions of the speaker. Similarly, the parent of a kidnapped child might make an *emotional* plea for the child's return. An *emotive* issue is one that generally bypasses logic and reason and goes straight to the emotions. It is probably intent on raising the listener's emotions, rather than displaying the speaker's genuine feelings.

Enquiry/Inquiry

American English doesn't seem to make a distinction between these two and British English seems to be following suit. *Enquiry* means asking about something in general terms, whereas an *inquiry* is a form of investigation (you have an *Official Inquiry* into something). If in doubt, *enquire* is probably better, but it really doesn't matter that much.

Envelop/Envelope

Envelop is a verb meaning to *wrap up, cover, conceal* or, in military terms, *to surround an enemy*. An *envelope* is an *outer casing* of some kind, most often of a letter.

Extant/Extinct

Nasty one this, as they mean the opposite of one another. *Extant* means *still in existence*, whereas *extinct* means *no longer in existence* (as in the dodo), or *no longer active* (as in volcanoes) or *dead*.

Faint/Feint

Faint has several meanings. Its most common meaning is to do with being *dim* or *indistinct* or *lightly drawn in*. My exercise book has *faint* lines (rather than bold ones). It can mean *swooning* —

in bad romances, the heroine *faints*. It can also mean something along the lines of *remote* or *slight*, as in *There was a **faint** glimmer of hope that there might be survivors*. *Feint* is to do with pretence. When you *feign* something, such as an attack or a punch, then this is a *feint*.

Fictional/Fictitious

Both these words are concerned with the creating of stories. If something is *fictional*, it is made up, or at best part true. Tom Sawyer is *fiction*. Robinson Crusoe is a *fictional* account supposedly based on the adventures of Alexander Selkirk. *Fictitious* is far more negative, it implies lying and deceitfulness. *He gave officers a **fictitious** name and address. The MP submitted **fictitious** expenses.*

Flair/Flare

Flair is concerned with talent or ability. *She has a **flair** for languages. He has a **flair** for knowing exactly what the public wants.* *Flare* is for all other meanings of the word, including *widening* (as in *flared* trousers), *bright lights* and *matches*.

Flammable/Inflammable/Non-flammable

Flammable and *inflammable* look as though they should mean the opposite of one another, but they don't. They mean exactly the same thing — that something has a *propensity to burst into flames*. *Flammable* is now emerging as the preferred option, probably to avoid confusion. *Non-flammable* is the opposite of both words.

Flaunt/Flout

This is a common mistake. If you *flaunt* something, you're showing off. *Flout* is normally used in the set expression *flout the rules*, i.e., *break the rules*.

Flounder/Founder

These two words tend to become confused when they are used in the context of watery accidents. A ship *founders* on a rock, whereas a drowning man *flounders*. *Flounder* means *struggle to move*. If you remember the *fl-* of someone *flapping* around, it helps you differentiate between the two words.

For ever/Forever

I'm always getting this wrong. Frankly, there is less and less distinction between the two uses. I asked a clever friend with a degree in English from Cambridge if she knew the difference and she didn't, so why should we? In theory when you mean *forever* as in *constantly/repeatedly/often*, then you should use *forever*. *Writers are **forever** being asked where they get their ideas.* If, on the other hand, you mean for eternity, then you need *for ever*. *I will love you **for ever**.*

Former/Latter

Laurel and Hardy were a popular comedy duo. The *former* was slim; the *latter* rotund. These terms feel old-fashioned. People use them to avoid repetition, but everyone always has to puzzle out who you're really referring to and you stand a chance that they (or you) will get it wrong. It's a good idea to find a way of working round the problem. *Laurel and Hardy were a popular comedy duo. Laurel was slim; Hardy rotund.*

Gender/Sex

There is the kind of idiot who, when filling out an official form, thinks that when he gets to the little box marked *sex*, writing 'yes, please' is the height of wit. If you are in the situation where the term *sex* is going to be misinterpreted as the act of coitus, then use the word *gender*. It stops this kind of stupid reply. *Sex* and *gender* can be used interchangeably when they mean *gender*. On the other hand, nobody rushes home because they've been promised *gender* tonight.

Gourmand/Gourmet

Both of these are French words. A *gourmand* is essentially someone who likes to eat a lot, it's not quite gluttony, more like *having a hearty appetite*. When I was a child, this was known as being a 'good trencherman', a noble expression you rarely hear nowadays. A *gourmet* likes fine dining.

Grill/Grille

A *grill* is what you cook on or can be used in a more general sense for a restaurant that serves grilled food. You find a *grille* on the front end of a motorcar, a grating or the bars on a window.

Hanged/Hung

Both are past participles of the verb hang. *Hanged* is used for people when they are executed. William Palmer was *hanged* at Stafford Gaol. Everything else is *hung*, including pheasants.

Hear/Here

Hear is to do with sound, *here* to do with place. Generally, people don't mix them up apart from when they mistype one for another. You do occasionally come across misuse when a word is used in a set phrase, such as *in the **here** and now*. Similarly, **Hear, hear** is what politicians cry when they shout out agreement.

Historic/Historical

An *historic* event (note that it's *an* not *a*) is an event of importance that took place in the past. The Battle of Hastings is *historic*.

It changed the way the country was ruled. *Historical* refers to anything that took place in the past regardless of importance.

Human/Humane

Human is the adjective relating to people, as in *human beings*. *Humane* means kind or decent.

Imperial/Imperious

Imperial is the adjective from the noun *empire*. Thus, we have *imperial* thrones or *imperial* armies. Although *imperious* has the same root, it tends to describe someone rather unpleasant and condescending. You find the word often in set phrases, such as *imperious command* or *imperious tones*.

Impinge/Infringe

These two words mean almost the same thing: more-or-less the same as *encroach*. They're both often used in the phrase *impinge on someone's privacy/infringe someone's privacy*. *Infringe* is stronger than *impinge* as it carries the additional sense of *rule-breaking* or *violation*. If you're not sure which to use, then perhaps it's best to *encroach* on someone's privacy, just in case you're accidentally overstating the case.

Imply/Infer

There's a great scene in an episode of the Inspector Morse when his pettifogging boss says something along the lines of, 'Are you trying to *infer* I'm stupid?' To which Morse replies, 'No, I'm *implying* it.' If your doctor asks you if you have thought about a weight-reduction eating plan, he's probably *implying* you are carrying a few excess pounds. If your neighbour gets a promotion and suddenly a Bentley appears in the driveway and they build a two-storey extension the size of a small palace, you can *infer* that the promotion came with a decent pay-rise. *Infer* is almost the same as *deduce*.

Inapt/Inept

Inapt means *not apt*, in other words *not correct for the purpose intended*. A spanner is an *inapt* tool for turning screws. It is often used in the set phrase *inapt remark*, which again means that the speaker has said something inappropriate. *Inept* means incompetent, or sometimes clumsy. If a workman arrived and tried to tighten a screw with a spanner, you would know he was *inept*.

Ingenious/Ingenuous

Ingenious means *clever* or *skilful*. Inventions are often described as *ingenious*. *Ingenuous* means something along the lines of *gullible* or *credulous*. If a person is *ingenuous*, it implies that they will easily believe something, that they are particularly *naïve* or *credulous*.

Interment/Internment

Interment means putting something into the ground — in other words a burial. *Internment* is when you lock someone up, for instance in an *internment* camp.

Junction/Juncture

A *junction* is a point at which two things meet. It is often used for railway stations where two or more lines join up — Crewe is a major *railway junction*. It's used for roads too. *Spaghetti Junction* is the nickname for the Gravelly Hill Interchange where the Aston Expressway meets the M6 in a series of clever loops. You also get *junction boxes* in electrical work. Although *juncture* can mean the same as *junction* in certain specific circumstances, it is most often used to mean a *crisis point*. *We cannot make any further progress at this* **juncture** *(*not *at this* **junction***)*.

Knew/New

Knew is the past form of the verb *know*. *New* means *fresh, unused*. That's dead obvious, really. I only included it as it's a common typo.

Know/No

As is this.

Lay/Lie

Let's deal with these two without getting smutty. Strictly speaking *lay* is a transitive verb, in other words, you *lay* something, such as *lay a table, lay down the rules, lay a blanket on the ground*. If you do it to yourself, then you should use *lie* and its variants. *I was **lying** on the bed when I heard a shout*. The difference may be being eroded, but again it's one of those little grammatical niggles that get under the skin of purists.

Lend/Loan

Both words are concerned with borrowing. *Lend* should be the verb and *loan* the noun, but American English uses *loan* as a verb, so inevitably we're shifting towards this use. Theoretically, you should write: *can you lend me a tenner?* but *the tenner I gave him was a loan*. However, we're getting to see more phrases such as *this picture has been loaned by the Guggenheim Museum*. Perhaps it doesn't matter at all.

Libel/Slander

Both are forms of *defamation*, which essentially means stating something disparaging, but untrue, about a living person.

Slander is for the spoken form, *libel* for the published or recorded form.

Licence/License

The easiest way to remember which way to spell this is to think of *advice/advise* which sound different when spoken aloud. *Advice* (which has a C) is the noun. *Advise* (with -S) is the verb. It's the same with *licence* and *license*. Only the noun needs a C, and even then only in British English. You have a *driving licence*. The pub has a *licence to sell alcohol*. This makes you *licensed to drive* and them *licensed to sell beer* under the *licensing laws*.

Lightening/Lightning

Lightening means to *make lighter*, both in the sense of *reducing weight* and of *introducing brightness*. *Lightning* is what you get during an electrical storm.

Loose/Lose

The double-o of *loose* is the sound to latch onto here, the *ooh*-sound. That makes it *loose*, i.e., not tight. You *lose* socks, weight, patience and custody battles.

Meter/Metre

A *meter* is a device that measures something. We have *electricity meters* and *gas meters* and *thermometers* (thermo-meters). A *metre* is an actual unit of measurement, a little over a yard long. It is divided into *centimetres*, similarly a thousand *metres* is a *kilometre*.

Militate/Mitigate

Militate means to *oppose* or to *fight*. It is usually followed by the word against. *What you're saying **militates** against everything I* *have learned before. Mitigate*, which is sometimes used by mistake for *militate*, means to make something *less severe*. *His grief at the loss of his dog was **mitigated** by the fact that he was soon shacked up with a bride twenty years his junior.* You will often hear the term *mitigating circumstances*, which means that there are reasons for the Judge to go easy on you.

Momentary/Momentous

Momentary means *lasting for a moment. It was a **momentary** act of madness.* It implies something *brief, split-second, short-lived. Momentous* means *having great importance.* Nelson Mandela's release from prison and the fall of the Berlin Wall were *momentous* events.

Moral/Morale

Moral is to do with the *goodness and badness* of the human character. *Moral sense*, for instance, is the ability most of us have to distinguish between right and wrong. *Moral* is also used to describe the point of a story, such as a parable, or one of Aesop's fables. *Morale* is to do with one's *mental well-being. The boss gave us all a pay-rise, which was good for **morale**.*

Official/Officious

Official is the adjective from office. A *railway official* is a person working for the railway, whose authority comes from the job they're doing. An *official delegation* will be a group of people who have authority vested in them by whatever body they represent. You'll also find the word official used in set phrases such as *official opening of parliament, official state banquet.* In these cases, there is probably also a touch of ceremony about the occasion. If your *railway official* becomes *officious*, that means that they're behaving in a *petty, authoritarian* way. An officious person is occasionally referred to as a *jobsworth* — they fuss over details and often adhere strictly to the rules without having the mental capacity to know when these should be bent or broken.

Passed/Past

Passed is from the verb *pass*, which has shed loads of meanings. *He **passed** his examinations. She **passed** by on the other side of the street. The old woman **passed** away. The House of Commons **passed** a new law. Time **passed** slowly. He **passed** the ball out to the wing. We **passed** the lorry. We heard the conversation that **passed** between the two criminals. Past* refers to time gone by and thus can also be used in expressions such as *past-master* or *past pupil* (meaning *former* or *ex* -). You'll come across it in set phrases such as *I wouldn't put it **past** him. Past* is also used as a preposition, often meaning either *in front of* or *beyond. I walked **past** the butcher's shop. By this stage, he was **past** caring. It's **past** the Post Office, then third turning on the left. March-**past**.*

Peace/Piece

Peace means *quietness* or *tranquillity* or a *cessation of hostilities*. Use *piece* for all the other meanings.

Pedal/Peddle

You *pedal* a bike or put your foot on the *accelerator pedal* of a car or the *sustain pedal* on the piano. In theory, you shouldn't write *foot pedal* as the *ped* bit comes from the Latin and means *foot* anyway. You *peddle* goods or ideas. *Peddle* also sometimes has the connotation of *selling goods illegally*, such as drugs or arms.

Plain/Plane

You're almost sure to know the difference; it's just a common typing error. *Plain* is normally used as an adjective where it can mean a host of things from *not good-looking*, normally sexist, (*she was a bit of a **plain Jane***) to undecorated (*she liked the walls of her house to be **plain***) or straightforward (*Writing Good, **Plain English***). *Plane* is often short for *aeroplane* and can also refer to a small hand-tool used for smoothing off surfaces. It can also mean *level* or *tier* as in *she's on a completely different **plane** to the rest of us*. Where the most confusion arises is where we have the mathematical term *plane*, which refers to a *smooth or level surface*. But we also have *plain* meaning a level area of countryside, such as *Salisbury **Plain*** or the *rain in Spain, which is mainly in the **plains***.

Populace/Populous

The *populace* are the people who live in a place. *Populous* means that many people live there. Tokyo is a *populous* city.

Practice/Practise

Practice is the noun. For many years she ran a successful dental *practice*. *Practise* is the verb. He *practised* hard and became a skilled player. Use the sound of *advice/advise* as a way of remembering the *C/S* spelling, as with *licence/license*.

Precede/Proceed

These two are easy to confuse because when we say them aloud, there is little difference in sound. *Precede* means to go before. Again, you have the prefix *pre-* (meaning *before*) to help you out. *The Lord Mayor was **preceded** into the room by the Duchess of Scunthorpe*. In other words, the Duchess went in *before* the Lord Mayor. *Proceed* just means to *go forward* or *go along*. *I was **proceeding** along Main Street when I was set upon by two drunken gentlemen.*

Prescribe/Proscribe

A doctor *prescribes* a medicine. *Prescribe* is the verb from the noun *prescription*. *Proscribe* means more-or-less the same as *prohibit*. The shared prefix of *proscribe* and *prohibit* (*pro-*) should help you remember.

Principal/Principle

Principal, as an adjective means *of primary importance. Our* **principal** *concern is for the welfare of the child.* As a noun, a *principal* is *head of an organisation*, e.g., a *college principal*. A *principle* is a *fundamental truth, proposition, standard* or *law. It is against her* **principles** *to eat meat.*

Procrastinate/Prevaricate

Nasty one this, because whilst you might live with being accused of *procrastination* (*putting work off till tomorrow*) you certainly don't want to be told you're *prevaricating*. Essentially, *prevaricate* is a clever word for *lying*. Even more importantly, never accuse a *procrastinator* of *prevaricating*. It could end up in court (see *libel/slander*). Rule-of-thumb: don't use the word *prevaricate*.

Program/Programme

Program is essentially the American spelling of the word *programme*. However, it is normally used as a computing term. Microsoft Office is a computer *program*, although the term *app*, short for application, seems to be taking over. On the other hand, the Archers is a radio *programme* and Panorama a TV *programme*. When you get to variations of the word, it's probably better usage to use a double *–m*: *computer programmer, programmed, programming,* even though American usage seems to allow a single *–m*.

Quite/Quiet

This is another entry to flag up typical typos. You know that *quiet* means *peaceful* or *not noisy or busy. I had a **quiet** day at work today. Quite* is normally uses as a weak intensifier. *The play was **quite** interesting.*

Racket/racquet

You use a *racquet* in tennis, badminton and so forth. All other meanings of the word use *racket*. Dodgy scams and loud behaviour are both *rackets*.

Rein/Reign/Rain

Rein is what you attach to a bridle to control a horse. If you use the expression, *giving someone free rein*, it means that they can do what they like. *Reign* is what a monarch does, and *rain* is what falls out of the sky. In this country, that seems to happen only on the days when we don't have snow or sleet.

Seam/Seem

Seam has to do with where two edges meet, such as in dressmaking. You also have *coal seams* and *seam bowlers. Seem* means *appear to be. He **seemed** very pleasant until he opened his mouth.*

Sew/So/Sow

Again, this is largely here to flag up typos. *Sew* is, to paraphrase the song, what you do with a *needle and thread*. It's also the spelling you need if you *sew up a deal. Sow* is used for when you *scatter seeds on the ground*, and by association, you can *sow seeds in people's minds*, or *sow doubt* in them for that matter. *Sow* (with a different pronunciation) is also a female pig and the name of a river. *So* has many different definitions that there's not space enough for them here. Let's just say that it's *so* for more-or-less all the other variations.

Shear/Sheer

Shear means something along the lines of cut or break. The bolt *sheared* off the engine. He works as a *sheepshearer*. *Sheer* is for everything else — *sheer cliffs, sheer drops, sheer good luck, sheer tights, sheer hype.*

Simple/Simplistic

People seem to be using *simplistic* more and more, when really they mean *simple*. *Simple* implies something easy or straightforward or elementary. *Simple* arithmetic might involve adding and subtracting. *Simple* accounts would be less detailed than full-blown company accounts. *Simplistic* is most often used when dealing with complex issues. For instance, if we examine crime and say that it is caused because some people are naughty, this is a *simplistic* explanation. There are so many factors that come into account (education, background, poverty, the general state of the economy, population density, mental health etc.) that attributing criminality to a single cause would be *simplistic*.

Stationery/Stationary

So easily confused. I was taught at school that 'E is for envelope'. *Stationery* includes paper, pens, pencils, scissors, notebooks and – of course – envelopes. *Stationary* is something standing still, such as a *stationary* vehicle.

Suit/Suite

Suit is used for clothing or cards – spades, diamonds, clubs and hearts are *suits*. A *suite* is a set of rooms (often in a hotel), or furniture that matches – most commonly a three-piece *suite*. Occasionally, you'll find it used for some forms of orchestral music where the individual parts make up a greater whole. *Peer Gynt* by Grieg is a *suite*, as is Holst's *The Planets*.

Their/There/They're

Say all three together and you'll sound as though you're comforting a distressed child. *Their* means belonging to them. It's *their* house. *There* indicates place. I put my book down over *there*. *They're* is a contraction of *they are*. And yes, whilst writing this little section, I managed to type them all wrong. I'm sure we all know what they mean, it's just so easy to write down the wrong spelling.

To/Too/Two

Just like *their/there/they're*, we probably know this, but writing quickly makes us get it wrong. *To* is a preposition. I am going *to* the shops. *Too* often means *as well*. Can I come *too*? It is also used to mean excessively. *I'm not going, it's **too** far*. *Two* is a number (2).

Toe/Tow

You wouldn't believe people get this wrong, but according to the Guardian newspaper, it's the fourth commonest written confusion. It's probably never confused when someone is generally referring to the bits on the end of their feet; those are your *toes*. We also know that if your car breaks down you need a *tow*. Where the most confusion comes is in the set expression *toe the line*. The derivation of the phrase is supposed to be from the way athletes line up in a race, with their toes on the line, which makes it easier to remember which spelling to use.

Who's/Whose

Who's is a contracted form of who is. **Who's** *sorry now?* = Who is sorry now? *Whose* is a possessive. **Whose** *house is this?* = To whom does this house belong?

Your/You're

Your is possessive, *you're* is short for you are. So, *you're* the cream in my coffee, but I wanna be *your* man.

8

A Quick Guide to English Grammar

In this section, we're going to take a look at grammar and especially at what they call 'Parts of Speech'. What I've written here is meant as a quick tour. It's not meant as a replacement for a comprehensive guide to the subject. Nor is grammar the world's most riveting topic. If you attempt to read this at one sitting, you will need a pot of strong coffee and more will power than you can imagine.

Grammar has got itself a bad name, as we've already seen. What happened in the past was that this general theory of language became translated into an immutable set of rules. This is what made grammar such tedious, hard work. This isn't helped by the fact that grammar is always dealt with out of context (including here). You have to have little examples, which are often detached from any real meaning.

The good news is that contrary to what you might have been told at school, you don't have to have a massive in-depth knowledge of grammar to write well. But, as I've already mentioned, it is useful to have a passing knowledge of a fistful of basic grammatical terms, such as nouns, adjectives, verbs, etc. Don't be frightened by the terminology, or by the fact that you never mastered French verbs at school. Pompous grammar bores nearly always get things wrong anyway.

Grammar is a kind of theory of language based on generalisations. It's an attempt to understand the structure of languages in a systematic way. I often hear people saying that they're no good at grammar. I suspect what they mean is that they don't know the terminology. All of us are incredibly good at grammar. We absorb it from the world around us, even if we can't tell a noun from a preposition.

You can see this with small children. When they begin speaking, they gradually learn the conventions of grammar — the way in which words work. Sometimes, they apply these conventions slightly wrongly.

Mummy goed to work yesterday.

Here, the child has got the word order right and has also learnt that if you add *-ed* on the end of a verb, we're talking about an event in the past. It works for *play/played, watch/watched, listen/listened.* It doesn't work for *go, eat* or *ride,* for instance. So the child's got the general concept, but is not at the stage yet where they've learnt some of the more subtle variations:

Mummy went to work yesterday. (not **goed**)
I ate a peach last week. (not **eated**)
She rode upon a donkey. (not **rided**)

But we know what the child means and we can tell that they are moving towards an understanding of the way language works. It is amazing how brilliant children are at grammar by the time they get to primary school.

When we talk about grammar, we're also usually referring to two different elements. There is syntax, which looks at the way in which words are combined — how word combinations and the order in which they occur make sense. If we write:

Steak the man the tomorrow eat barbecue going is at to

Here, we've just got a string of words. Yoda in Star Wars has the same sort of random approach to word order. Give it some sensible shape and we have:

The man is going to eat steak at the barbecue tomorrow.

Then there is morphology, which is concerned with the actual internal structure of words themselves.

Knowledge of English morphology would include understanding that the plural of the word *dog* is *dogs,* or that if we want to talk in the past tense, we have to alter most verbs, as we've already seen. So if we refer to something that we used to like, but no longer do, we would change the word *like* to *liked.*

We're actually lucky with English in that it doesn't inflect a great deal — we don't get many variations of a word. Even one of the slipperiest verbs in English, *to be,* has only 7 further variations: *am, are, is, was, were, being, been.*

Its equivalent in French, *être,* has the following variations: *suis, es, est, sommes, êtes, sont, été, étant, étais, était, étions, étiez, étaient, fus, fut, fûmes, fûtes, furent, serai, seras, sera, serons, serez, seront, serais, serait, serions, seriez, seraient, sois, soit, soyons, soyez, soient, fusse, fusses, fût, fussions, fussiez, fussent.*

If I've counted correctly, and not missed any, I make that 41 variations in all. Similarly, whilst there are a few plurals in English that don't follow the general flow – *sheep/sheep, knife/ knives, fish/fish, lady/ladies,* or *child/children,* most of them just add an *-s.*

Then there are words such as *who/whom* or *he/him/himself.* For example, we change *he* to *him,* when *he* becomes the object of the sentence.

He *gave Mary an unpleasant disease.*

He is the subject: he does the giving.

*Mary gave **him** an unpleasant disease.*

He is now the object — Mary's doing the giving — so *he* has to change to **him**.

What was happening back in grammar-thumping days was that the old, fussy grammarians were trying to force English to match the systems they had for Latin. English is a Germanic language, so it was never going to work properly.

All languages have their own problems. For the foreign-language learner of English, one of the trickiest aspects is the little phrasal verbs we use all the time. For instance, *was up,* could be used in several different ways:

I was up in time for breakfast	*I had risen in time ...*
After I got my result, I was up	*I was pleased*
I was up to no good	*I was being naughty*
If it was up to me	*If it were my decision*

You can probably think of other examples. Native speakers normally cope with this easily enough. Indeed, the potential for misunderstanding often gives comedians plenty of mileage. An ancient, creaking example of this kind of double entendre is that *knock up* could mean *wake someone in the morning* or *get someone pregnant.*

However, in all, our grammar system is pretty easy, as is proven by those primary school children, who speak English like natives. So, without more ado, let's have a little look at some of the more useful grammatical terminology.

Parts of Speech and Other Useful Bits of Grammar

English is, obviously enough, made up of words. In sentences, words have different functions. Some of these terms you may recognise from schooldays, especially if you learned a foreign language. They are the essential building blocks of language. A little knowledge of the structure of language is useful. However, you don't have to overdo it. Here we're just concerned with basics, so don't panic. I've tried to keep the information to a minimum, so if you're a grammar fiend already, you're bound to spot things you think I should have included.

Context is Everything

As with all grammatical terms, you can only say with certainty what part of speech a word is by its context — the way in which it is used in a sentence.

*I gave her a **box** of **chocolates**.*

Here, both *box* and *chocolates* are nouns. They are the names we give to tangible things. However, if we write:

*I am going to **box** the world heavyweight champion next week.*

The word *box* is now a verb.

*I gave her a **chocolate** Easter egg.*

Chocolate now describes the egg (as does the word Easter), so it is being used as an adjective.

We use the term parts of speech to categorise the different basic functions of words. Parts of speech include nouns, adjectives, verbs, adverbs and so forth. So let's see how some of these work.

Nouns

A noun is a naming word. It is used for classifying places, things, people and animals, and ideas/concepts. For example in the following sentence, we have two nouns:

*Peter is a good **boy**.*

Peter names a person. *Boy* is the name we give to a type/ category of human being.

Look at the next example and see if you can decide which words are nouns. There are four in total:

The trouble with my brother is that he always wants to use my car when I'm away on holiday.

With luck, you will have spotted that *trouble*, *brother*, *car* and *holiday* are nouns. If you didn't get it straight away, don't worry, it will come with practice. When we sub-divide nouns further, we get six types of noun. They are really three sets, further divided into two opposites. We have proper nouns and common nouns, concrete nouns and abstract nouns, countable nouns and uncountable nouns. Most nouns fit into more than one set. Think of them as overlapping categories, it makes life a little easier. Let's look at each in turn:

Proper Nouns

Proper nouns are essentially just the actual names of places, people, towns, rivers. Normally you need to spell these with a capital letter:

Sicily, Paris, Brazil, Ethel, Charles Dickens, Ben Nevis, Kurt Wallander

Common Nouns

This means everything else (except proper nouns) that is a noun:

Beauty, truth, house, boy, car, elephant, school, motorway, pilot, oven, sentiment

Concrete Nouns

These are things you can touch (even if only in theory):

Boy, car, elephant, motorway, pilot, beer, river, casserole, eyeball

Abstract Nouns

These are the names of concepts – things you can't touch:

Beauty, hatred, destiny, truth, honesty, integrity

Countable nouns

These can be put in the plural – in other words, you can (theoretically at least) count them:

River/rivers, shed/sheds, Jones/Joneses, elephant/elephants

Uncountable Nouns

And, yes, that's right. You can't pluralise these:

Independence (you can't have independences*), traffic* (no such thing as *traffics* when referring to roads/trains or whatever). Of course, some nouns are sometimes countable and sometimes uncountable. For example, if you're referring to *beauty* as a concept, then you can't pluralise it to *beauties*, whereas you might refer to the fabulous tomatoes you have grown as *beauties*.

Verbs

Verbs are 'doing' words:

*He **ate** a lot of fish.*
*I **used to enjoy** cowboy films.*
*Every year, we **go** to France on holiday.*
*There **are** fairies at the bottom of the garden.*
*He **drinks** more than **is** good for him.*
*Just **think** what we **could do**!*

Note that sometimes verbs just consist of one word (*He **ate** fish*). We call these simple verbs. At other times, we need more than one word (*I **used to enjoy** cowboy films*) and these are called compound verbs. So, for example the verb clusters in:

*I **am going** to the cinema*
*She **has eaten** everything on the menu*

… are compound verbs. They combine two verbs. The main verbs in the above examples are variations on the words *go* (*going*) and *eat* (*eaten*). They are helped by what we call auxiliary verbs. In the first example, the word *am* is the auxiliary verb. *Am* is from the verb *to be*. In our second example, the word *has*, from the verb *to have*, is the auxiliary.

The word 'tense' really refers to time. Although there are twelve tenses in English, I won't go into all twelve here. That said, it is useful to know that they are grouped into three sets – past, present and future. Basic examples of these might be:

> She **likes** a drop of red wine. (*Likes* is present)
> We **went** to Egypt last year. (*Went* is past)
> Your parcel **will arrive** on Thursday. (*Will arrive* is future)

Passive and Active Voice

Using the *active* voice tends to make better writing than using the *passive*. But before we look at what *active* and *passive* mean, let's just clarify what we mean by the *subject* and *object* of a sentence. If we take a simple sentence such as:

Penny ate dinner

Penny is the **subject** of the sentence. She's doing the actual eating. *Ate* is the verb, the doing word. She's not *burning* dinner, she's *eating* it. *Dinner* is the **object**. It's what's getting eaten (or burned for that matter).

If we change the sentence around, we get:

The dinner was eaten by Penny.

Penny is still technically the subject of the sentence – she is still doing the eating, but the voice has changed from active (Penny *ate*) to passive (the dinner *was eaten*).

Active	Passive
The car hit the pedestrian	*The pedestrian was hit by a car*
The arsonist burnt the house down	*The house was burnt down by the arsonist*

Finite and Non-finite Verbs

It's also handy to be able to differentiate between **finite** and **non-finite** verbs.

A **finite** verb needs a subject:

I play football at the weekends.

The subject here is *I*.

A **non-finite** verb is generally either a form of the infinitive (to + verb):

to go, to sleep, to eat, to drive, to relax, to shave

Or it might be a variation of the present participle when it is used as an adjective or a noun:

Going *on holiday is fun.*

*Let **sleeping** dogs lie.*

*No **eating** in the staffroom.*

If we take one present participle as a little example – *playing* – we can see that it is sometimes part of a finite verb:

*I am **playing** football.*

It has a subject (*I*). However, the moment you use it as an adjective or noun, it is now a non-finite verb:

Playing *football is good fun.*

*I was injured whilst **playing** football.*

Adjectives

An adjective is a describing word. Yes, you remember that from French at school, as well.

The *red* tractor.

The *long* and *winding* road.

The *parliamentary* candidate for *Greater* Manchester.

You'll also find that groups of words can have the same function as a single adjective. In the Beatles' song title above, we have two words describing the same noun – *long* and *winding*.

When we get an entire phrase or clause describing a noun, these are called adjectival phrases or adjectival clauses, depending on whether they're phrases or clauses naturally enough:

The house I visited last June is still up for sale.

I visited last June is an adjectival clause describing the house. *Still up for sale* also describes the house. It is an adjectival phrase (there's no finite verb in it).

Comparatives and Superlatives of Adjectives

We've already touched on this. You can use variations on a basic adjective to describe how things or people relate to another. For example:

*I have an **older** sister and a **younger** brother.*
*The mattress on the bed is the **firmest** she could find.*
*It was the **largest** pork pie he had ever seen.*

The words *older* and *younger* are comparative forms of adjectives; *firmest* and *largest* are superlatives.

The comparative is used when you compare two items or people.

Manchester is a large city. London is also a large city.
*London is the **larger**.*
*Mr Smith is rich. Mrs Jones is rich. Mrs Jones is **richer** than Mr Smith.*

Superlatives are needed when you have three or more items. For example, if you write *I am the **oldest** child*, it should mean that there are at least three of you.

*Manchester is a large city. Birmingham is even larger, but London is the **largest** city in the UK.*
*Mr Smith is rich. Mr Jones is very rich. Mr Edwards is the **richest** of them all.*

Most comparative adjectives end in –r or –er:

Bigger smaller richer poorer

...and most superlatives end in –est:

Biggest richest oldest poorest

Some require a bit of sleight of hand with the spelling:

Lovely Lovelier Loveliest

There are also several irregular versions, including:

Good better best

Bad worse worst

Little less least

Much more most

And, of course, sometimes you can't change the adjective at all and have to use *more* and *most*:

*I am honest. My wife is **more honest**. My MP is the **most honest** of all of us.*

Adverbs

An adverb is another kind of describing word. It does the same job with a verb as an adjective does with a noun. It describes how something is done. It often ends in '–ly':

*He drank his tea **quickly**.*

*She ate **noisily**.*

But it doesn't have to:

*She fell over **backwards** and he fell **sideways**.*

Sometimes you'll find a phrase or a clause used as an adverb:

*She always slept **with the light on**.*

With the light on describes how she slept. It is an adverbial phrase (it contains no finite verb).

*She always slept **more lightly than I did**.*

More lightly than I did is an adverbial clause (it contains a finite verb), but it also describes how she slept.

Pronoun

A pronoun is a word which stands in for a noun. For example:

John loves smoked salmon; **it** *is tasty.*

It refers to the smoked salmon.

The boys are back in town. **They** *are back in town.*

Her mother is coming to stay. **She** *is coming to stay.*

Commonly used pronouns include *I, you, he, she, it, they, we*
There are other kinds of pronouns, including:

Reflexive Pronouns

These refer to things you do to yourself. They always end in –*self*.

He cut **himself** *shaving.*

Enjoy **yourself**: *it's later than you think.*

Possessive pronouns

These denote ownership: *mine, yours, his, hers, its, ours, theirs.*

This is my book. It's **mine**.

The car parked outside belongs to my father. It's **his.**

Interrogative Pronouns

These are essentially question words, such as *who, what, where, whose, whom, which*. The answer must be a noun.

What *do you think you are doing?*

Who *is going to wash the kitchen floor?*

Demonstrative Pronouns

This, these, that and *those* are demonstrative pronouns.

This *is the best book I have ever read. (The book I am showing you is the best book I have ever read.)*

What on earth is **that**? *(Tell me what the object I'm pointing at is.)*

Prepositions

These are words and phrases that show us how two elements of a sentence are linked. Often these are to do with positions – in the widest sense – hence prepositions. *In, on, by, with, from, to, near to, because of, in front of, along* are all prepositions. For instance:

> She works **in** a bookshop.
> I live **by** the river.
> She's hoping to get a text **from** him.

Conjunctions

Conjunctions are words such as *and, although, because, or, but, however, if.* They join two halves of a sentence together.

> I am working today, **although** I have a nasty cold.
> She's going to lie down, **because** she's feeling tired.
> They're going to go to France **if** they can afford it.

Articles

Articles come in two varieties. *The* is the definite article. *A (or an)* is the indefinite article. This is easy to remember. If we refer to *the* banana, we know exactly which banana it is. We are talking about a specific banana – a definite banana.

> I have eaten **the** banana you gave me for lunch.

If we're not being specific, for instance, if we have a bunch of bananas in the fruit bowl, we'd be more likely to talk about *a* banana.

> I ate **a** banana for lunch.

In other words, I ate one of the bananas from the bowl. We are being indefinite, non-specific.

Frankly, that's quite enough grammar for one small paperback.

9

Cutting out the Waste, Keeping the Writing Tight

Earlier, we saw how much better writing sounds if you cut out Latinate words and trim flabby phrases. Here are some of the more common ones to think about. You might not agree with everything and, indeed, sometimes the longer word or phrase does make more sense, but the rule-of-thumb is *short good, long bad*.

As with all rules, there are exceptions. Besides, you sometimes genuinely need words to be a little bit squirmy. For instance, it should be better to write *cheap* instead of *less expensive*. However, if you're trying to do a deal, then *more affordable* and *less expensive* sound better than *cheap*. The word *cheap* carries connotations – are the goods shoddy or are you too tight-fisted to shell out for something better?

Long	Shorter or Easier Version
A proportion of	some
Accelerate	speed up
Accordingly	so
Adequate	(good) enough
Adjacent to	next to

Advantageous	better
Advise	tell
Alleviate	reduce/ease
Ameliorate	improve/get better
Approximately	about
Arrive at a decision	decide
Ascertain	learn/find out
Assistance	help
At a later date	later
At that point in time	then
At this moment in time	now
Attempt	try
Attributable to	because of/due to
Augment	increase
Avail oneself of	use
Beneficial	good/helpful
Bring to a conclusion	end
Close proximity	near/nearby
Commence	start/begin
Commencement	start/beginning
Compared with/to	than
Completion	end/finish
Component	part
Concerning	about
Concur with	agree with
Consequently	so/thus
Constitute	form/be part of
Constructed of	made of
Correspond with	write/email/phone
Currently	now
Demonstrate	show
Despite the fact that	although/though/despite

Disclose	tell
Discontinue	stop
Discrete	separate
Documentation	documents/paperwork
Dominant	main
Draw the attention of the	point out/remind reader to
Due to the fact that	because/as
Dwelling	house/home
Elucidate	explain
Emphasise	stress
Endeavour	try
Enquire	ask
Ensure	make sure
Establish	find out/know
Excluding	except/apart from
Expedite	speed up
Facilitate	make easier
Firstly	first
For the duration of	during
For the purpose of	to
Frequently	often
Further to our letter	following our letter
Generate	make/create/produce (unless it's electricity)
Give due consideration to	consider/think about
Give positive encouragement to	encourage
Illustrate	show
Implement (as a verb)	do/carry out
In accordance with	as/in line with
In addition to	also/besides/as well as
In advance of our meeting	before our meeting
In connection with	about

In excess of	more than
In order that	so (that)
In order to	to
In short supply	scarce/hard to find
In spite of the fact that	despite
In the event that	if
In the near future	soon
In the neighbourhood of	around/about
In the normal course of our procedure	normally/usually
In the vicinity of	near
In view of the fact that	as/because
Indicate	show
Inform	tell
Initiate	start
Irrespective of	despite
Is not in a position to	cannot/can't
It is apparent therefore that	so/obviously
Locate	find/place/put
Make an approach to	approach
Methodology	method(s)
Notify	let (a person) know/tell
Notwithstanding	despite/even if
On numerous occasions	often
On the grounds that	because
On the part of	for/by
One of the reasons	one reason
Permissible	allowed
Personnel	staff/people/team
Possess	own/have
Previous to	before
Principal	main

Prior to	before
Provided that	if/as long as
Purchase (verb)	buy
Regarding	about
Remunerate	pay
Render	make
Request	ask
Retain	keep
Statutory	legal
Subsequent to	after
Subsequently	later/then/afterwards
Sufficient	enough
Supplementary	extra
Terminate	end/stop/finish
Under preparation	being prepared
Utilise	use
Valued at	worth
Voice approval	approve
Ways and means	ways or means, but not both
We are in receipt of	we have received
We are not in a position to	we cannot/we are unable to
We are of the opinion	we think
We should be glad if you will kindly	please
With effect from	from
With the exception of	except
With respect to	about
With the result that	so/so that

10

A Quick Guide to Punctuation

As we saw earlier, punctuation is a way of making written words easier to read, so we don't end up with:

if i ran on endlessly for page after page never stopping to draw breath piling sentence upon sentence with nothing to tell you where this sentence ends and where the next begins you would quickly become very annoyed lose the thread of what im trying to say and feel alienated by me and so you might just want to get a pickaxe and embed it in some part of my anatomy with a cry of how can you treat me so disrespectfully by not punctuating properly and I would shout back hey don't hit me im doing the best I can then you would just do it again this time shouting more loudly smack smack smack thwack thwack thwack

That's why we have punctuation. It helps break up the text for the reader and gives it a shape. It flags up when someone is speaking and enables us to draw breath. Punctuation marks are the little road signs on the highways and by-ways of reading.

These are the main punctuation marks:

Full-stop	.
Colon	:
Semi-Colon	;
Comma	,
Question mark	?
Single Quotation mark	'.......'
Double Quotation Mark/inverted Commas	"......"
Exclamation Mark	!
Ampersand	&
Asterisk	*
Hyphen	- or — (- = en-dash, — = em-dash)
Ellipsis1 (dot, dot, dot)	...
Forward Slash/Oblique Stroke	/
Back Slash	\
Apostrophe (to show belonging)	'
Brackets	(parentheses) ( )
Square Brackets	[ ]
• Bullet points	

I'm not sure if emojis and emoticons count as punctuation, but here's one anyway ☺.

Let's examine each in turn and see how best to use them. However, it's worth noting that one of the real difficulties with punctuation is that it's not always fixed and rigid. There are certain conventions that are useful, although a lot of their use is determined by gut feeling.

Full stop.

End of a Sentence

You generally need a full stop (which is sometimes also called a period) at the end of a sentence. The difficulty is defining exactly what we mean by *sentence*. One of the best ways of deciding if you have a sentence is to check if you have a finite verb in what you've written.

Normally a sentence will be a statement, usually just containing one or two basic ideas:

I ran as fast as I could to catch the train.
The bellringers practised on Wednesday evenings.

Don't forget that indirect questions and instructions don't take a question mark, but a full stop:

He asked me if I understood what he meant.
I wondered if she was ever going to go home.
Turn the handle fully to open the door.

However, fragments count as sentences too. What's a fragment?

This is.
And this.
As is this.

Proper, full sentences are generally easy to spot. But occasionally, you'll find that you write two separate sentences and connect them with a comma:

Everton won't win the cup this year, Liverpool's chances are not great either.

You've essentially got two different ideas here. In this case, you could write:

Everton won't win the cup this year. Liverpool's chances are not great either.

If you find that this leaves you with sentences that feel childishly short, then by all means join them together with a conjunction, such as *and*:

Everton won't win the cup this year and Liverpool's chances are not great either.

Once you've typed in a full stop, you should normally leave a single space after it. Some of us have the old-fashioned typist's habit of hitting the space bar twice, so try to remember to use find/replace to sort it out.

Full Stops and Abbreviations

There was once a time when all abbreviations were given a full stop. This is falling out of fashion. It is perfectly acceptable to write BBC, NATO, EU, DNA, OK. It is worth bearing in mind that if an abbreviation is not well known, it's a good idea to explain it the first time you use it.

The use of acronyms is being abused, according to the chairman of LAGUNA (The League against the Use of Nonsensical Acronyms).

Also, don't forget that if your sentence ends with an abbreviation and you decide that you're going to use full stops, then there's no need for a sentence-end full stop as well.

In France, we travelled on the T.G.V.

However, the easiest solution is not to use full stops in abbreviations, unless they just don't look right without them or the house style insists on them.

Colon:

Colon and Lists

The full colon, i.e. one full stop over another, is often used to introduce bullet points:

The items on today's agenda will be:
- *Reporting systems*
- *Latest in-store promotions*
- *Staff training*
- *New staff discount scheme*

It can also introduce lists that are not bullet-pointed, such as:
This is what we are looking for: honesty, integrity, grit and determination.

You will occasionally see a colon and a dash (:-). used together as a way of introducing a list. It's not a great way of doing it, not least because nowadays people think of them mainly as emoticons, of which more later.

The Colon and Clarification

You can use a colon to help bring an explanation or a clarification to the first half of a sentence. For example:
We have one large difficulty at the moment: funding the project.
The train was late: signal failure at Crewe.

Colon and Quotations

You can use a colon to introduce a quotation:
As Churchill said: 'I have nothing to offer but blood, sweat, toil and tears.'
But as you could equally well do it with a comma, why bother?

169

Semi-Colon ;

If you don't know how to use the semi-colon, don't use it. It's a largely redundant piece of punctuation that seems left over from a by-gone age. If, for whatever reason, you insist on it, just use it for awkward lists where the number of commas surrounding additional information make the sentence hard to read. If you write:

Visitors to the exhibition included the Mayor of Casterbridge, Mr Michael Henchard, the Brontë sisters, Anne, Emily and Charlotte and the Famous Five, George, Julian, Dick, Anne and Timmy the dog.

Frankly it's confusing. How many people (plus dog) are there? If you know nothing of these people/characters, you could reckon that there are at least 16 and Timmy the dog. But Michael Henchard is the Mayor of Casterbridge. There are three Brontë sisters (Anne, Emily, Charlotte) and the Famous Five are George, Julian, Dick, Anne and, of course, Timmy the dog. I make that eight people/characters and one dog.

Here, you can use the semi-colon to help divide up the groups:

Visitors to the exhibition included the Mayor of Casterbridge, Mr Michael Henchard; the Brontë sisters, Anne, Emily and Charlotte; and the Famous Five, George, Julian, Dick, Anne and Timmy the dog.

In neatly balanced sentences, you can avoid using the word *because* by having a semi-colon:

The witch was toying with her broomstick; fearful that it might lose its magic powers.

You can also use it to link together two clauses that are closely related to one another.

Take a stroll along the promenade; the view is excellent.

However, in this last case, because the two clauses could stand independently, you could just as easily write:

Take a stroll along the promenade. The view is excellent.

Or:

Take a stroll along the promenade because the view is excellent.

A more modern approach, using the em-dash instead of the semi-colon might be:

Take a stroll along the promenade — the view is excellent.

Or any number of ways, including:

For an excellent view, take a stroll along the promenade.

In other words, you can almost always find a way round using the semi-colon, so unless you're 100% sure of what you're doing, stop using it; you know it makes sense.

Comma,

The Comma and Lists

The comma is often used to break up lists:

The wise men brought gold, frankincense and myrrh.
I have nothing to offer but blood, sweat, toil and tears.
A sleek, blue car shot round the bend.

The Oxford Comma

Normally, you don't need a comma before the word *and* if it is just being used to denote the last item in a list.

She wore jeans, sneakers and a t-shirt.
The wise men brought gold, frankincense and myrrh.

However, you can use it if you like.

She wore jeans, sneakers, and a t-shirt.
The wise men brought gold, frankincense, and myrrh.

It is useful if you want to stop something from being ambiguous, a bit like when we had all those Brontës and Famous Fives.

We went to see my parents, Elizabeth and Harry Nelson, and Charlie Smith.

The above sentence implies that the writer's parents are Elizabeth and Harry Nelson. If they're not, then we need to revert to using the semi-colon to help break up the list.

Question Mark?

Direct Questions

You should use the question mark where you have a direct question:

Where are the books I gave you?
How do you solve a problem like Maria?
When do you think he's likely to get here?

But, as we saw earlier, you shouldn't use a question mark if your question is indirect:

She asked him the whereabouts of the books she had given him.
She wanted to know how to solve a problem like Maria.
He needed to know when his friend would get there.

Uncertainty

If we don't know something for sure, then using a question mark is handy:

When Geoffrey Chaucer wrote 'The Canterbury Tales' (1340–1370?), he used Middle English.

Inverted Commas

Single Quotation mark '...' and Double Quotation Mark "..."

Inverted commas go round directly quoted speech.

First of all, let's deal with whether to use single or double quotation marks. In the main, I would be tempted to use single marks as it is just a little less cluttered on the page. Professional writers do this, certainly in Britain, although it varies in other countries. However, as long as you are consistent, it doesn't really matter. If you then quote within the dialogue, you can use double marks:

> *John said, 'The old boy by the bus stop shouted, "Help!" when I walked past.'*

Or vice versa:

> *John said, "The old boy by the bus stop shouted, 'Help!' when I walked past."*

Inverted commas in themselves aren't too difficult. Everything that is directly said goes inside them and starts with a capital letter. What is harder is how to deal with all the punctuation that surrounds them.

> *John said, 'The old boy was standing by the bus-stop again. He was eating a prawn sandwich.'*

Note that there is a comma just before we open the quotation marks and that everything inside the inverted commas is punctuated as normal. We also use a comma at the end of a speech if we then use a 'said' clause:

> *'The old boy was standing by the bus stop again. He was eating a prawn sandwich,' said John.*

So far, so good, but it gets trickier when you start breaking up the actual quotation with the speech attribution (i.e., who said it).

'The old boy was standing by the bus-stop again,' said John. 'He was eating a prawn sandwich.'

Note the comma for the first part, the *said* is in lower case. That's because it's part of the first sentence. The second part is a freestanding sentence.

If you have dialogue, give each new speaker a fresh paragraph:

'The old boy was standing by the bus-stop again,' said John. 'He was eating a prawn sandwich.'
'Where do you suppose he got that?' said Mary.

No need for an extra comma inside the speech marks as we have the question mark.

With longer dialogue, as long as it is clear who is speaking, you don't need to attribute every single speech.

'The old boy was standing by the bus-stop again,' said John. 'He was eating a prawn sandwich.'
'Where do you suppose he got that?' said Mary.
'How am I supposed to know?'
'There's no need to bite my head off! I was only asking.'

Another way round the problem of speech attribution is to write something along the lines of:

John started setting the table. 'The old boy was standing by the bus-stop again.'

or:

'Where do you suppose he got that?' Mary poured herself a pint of vodka.

We then know that it is John speaking. It also avoids the need for you to go searching for alternatives to the word *said*.

Inverted commas and Slang

You will also find people sometimes using quotation marks for slang expressions or foreign phrases:

> *When we got there, he gave us each a little "snifter" and some "nibbles".*
>
> *In Tangiers, we were happy to tuck into a "couscous royal".*

This seems a bit old-fashioned. We're more capable of dealing with slang expressions or foreign words within more formal writing nowadays. Using inverted commas tends to place too much emphasis on the word in question.

Exclamation Mark!

There has been an outburst of exclamation marks since swathes of the country lost the ability to understand irony or can only write with breathless excitement.

Writers, terrified that their readers can't understand that they're being a little tongue-in-cheek or have enjoyed something, smack them at the end of every sentence. One editor I know rejects any article that has an exclamation mark in it, referring to them as screamers, and another simply does a find/ replace on the computer.

> *We got to Paris!! It was tremendously exciting!!! In the evening, we saw a show!!!!! We ate a meal!!!!!!! The waiter didn't speak English!!*

Already the reader's eyes have glazed over. Is this the work of a six-year-old child or a fully-grown adult? An exclamation mark should show something being exclaimed:

> *'Look out!' he shouted.*
>
> *'That's brilliant!' she said.*

They're just about tolerable in a text message or a matey email, but normally avoid the exclamation mark, unless you are quoting someone directly. Yes, in theory there are other uses for it, but it always makes the writer look like an idiot. As F. Scott Fitzgerald pointed out, an exclamation mark is laughing at your own joke, which is considered bad manners.

Ampersand &

The ampersand is best used when it forms part of a name, for instance, for a company. It's perfectly fine to write:

I worked at Smith & Jones for two years.

In this context, the ampersand sign (&) is generally better than the plus sign (+), only because it is visually more distinctive.

I worked at Smith + Jones for two years.

However, it looks wrong if you use it to join two clauses:

I worked at Smith & Jones for two years & thoroughly enjoyed every minute.

Asterisk *

You know how to use the s*****g asterisk. Yes, one of its uses is to disguise swear words. Fine, if you think swear words need disguising. Another use is to highlight something, perhaps if you want to add a footnote. You'll also see it used in lists:

The following people have been given keys to the executive toilet:

John Fowler
*Guy Johnson **
George Bailey
*Elwood P. Dowd **

Scottie Ferguson
Linus Rawlings *
*Those marked * have also been issued with commemorative Egyptian cotton face cloth embroidered with the company logo.*

Hyphen/Dash - or —

Strictly speaking, there are two forms of the hyphen. One is the *em* dash, the other the *en* dash. They got these names for when printers needed to know the size of dash that was wanted. Was it the size of a capital M or N?

The Em Dash

This is the longer of the two and acts almost like a comma. Its use is becoming more and more popular. It should take up a bit more space on the page than the typical en dash (or hyphen):

He went to the window — no joy there — so he came back in and sat down.

It can also be used to indicate some kind of emphasis:

We went to Spain that summer — three times.

The em-dash is often also used to enclose an idea, where alternatively you might use brackets or commas.

Two cities — Sodom and Gomorrah — were damaged in the earthquake.

At a pinch, if you want to differentiate and your computer's not playing ball, you can use – for the Em dash.

Hyphen (en dash)

This is the little dash between words that joins them together. You'll also often see it used at the end of a line in printed books to even up the spacing, when the right-hand margin is justified.

It's slightly awkward to use, which may account for its current unpopularity. The Germans don't bother with them much. If they want to sell you a semi-automatic glass-cutting machine, they'll simply advertise it as a *Halbautomatischglasschneidenmaschine.*

The hyphen is dropping out of fashion. It's a shame, as it does serve a useful purpose. Imagine you are at an old-fashioned funfair (or fun-fair) and you see the following two signs outside neighbouring marquees. The first one declares:

Come and see the man-eating fish!

The second:

Come and see the man eating fish!

I know which I'd be more interested in.

If we take examples such as *Man-eating fish* or *million-dollar house,* we can apply a little test. Can we separate out the component adjectives and still make sense?

A man-eating fish is not a *man fish* or an *eating fish.* It is a *man-eating fish. A million-dollar house* is neither a *million house* nor a *dollar house.* It is a *million-dollar house.*

In these cases, the hyphen is useful. However, the hyphen can be a law unto itself. Some words can be spelled with or without a hyphen and, as we've seen with so much of the language, usage is constantly changing. A recent book I read kept on referring to *pretrial reports,* which threw me every time. *Pre-trial reports* helps the reader know where to place the stress. I recently wrote something in which I used the word *boy-friend* to find it edited to *boyfriend.* I was obviously being a bit old-fashioned (or oldfashioned?). It's not that long ago since *to-day* and *to-morrow* were hyphenated, instead of the *today* and *tomorrow* that most of us use now. Indeed, my spell-checker (or spellchecker) is happy with *spell-checker, spellchecker, to-day, today, to-morrow* and *tomorrow.*

178

Similarly, there's no reason why it should be *son-in-law*, but *next of kin*. The best rule-of-thumb (or rule of thumb) is to look it up in a good, recent dictionary.

Numbers

The most common use of hyphens is for numbers:
Thirty-nine Steps
Twenty-first birthday party
It's also used when you get numbers in compound phrases:
Five-o'clock shadow

Hyphen or No Hyphen, Depending on Use

Note that often the adjectival variation requires hyphens:
*I found an **out-of-order** toilet,*
but when it's a separate clause or phrase:
*I found a toilet that was **out of order**.*

Differentiating between Similar Words

Hyphens also differentiate when you've got a word that would have a different meaning if it weren't hyphenated, such as with *re-count* (to count again), rather than *recount*, (to tell a story).
The vote was such a close call that the candidates demanded a **re-count**.
*He **recounted** his tales of derring-do in the polar wastes.*
Re-cover, to cover again, but *recover,* to regain something or to get better.
*The sofa needed **re-covering** with new material.*
*He caught the flu, but soon **recovered**.*

Separating Vowel Sounds

When you're going to get two vowels together, making it easier for the reader to spot where the join comes.

Co-owner, re-enrol, re-enlist, semi-automatic, semi-independent, co-operate, anti-oxidant.

Words that Start with a Solo Letter

A-level, U-boat, V-neck, X-ray, Y-chromosome

Ellipsis (dot, dot, dot) ...

This can be a handy device.

Leaving out Information

For instance, if you quote someone, but need to leave a chunk out, you can write:

Plots have I laid ...to set my brother Clarence and the king in deadly hate the one against the other.

As a Form of Pause

This can be especially useful in dialogue:

'So where were you on the night of the fifth?'
'I was ... I was ... watching television.'

And if you run out of steam and you can't go on, then just use three little dots ... But don't add a full stop after an ellipsis.

Forward Slash or Oblique Stroke / and the Backslash \

The forward slash tends to denote that the reader is going to take their pick of two items:

Use 125 grams/4 ½ oz. of sugar.
The reader might like to pause for a moment and consider his/her options.

And you might also use it for something along the lines of:
The shop had a bright red open/closed sign.

Poetry Line Breaks

If you don't display poetry with its original line breaks, then you use the oblique stroke to show where the breaks should be:

> *To be, or not to be, that is the question:/Whether 'tis Nobler in the mind to suffer/The Slings and Arrows of outrageous Fortune,/Or to take Arms against a Sea of troubles...*

Web References

The forward slash is also used in URLs, unlike the *Backslash* (\), which is a different beast altogether. It tends to be used in some computer commands.

Apostrophe '

This is the punctuation mark that often causes the most anguish, but it is simpler to use than most people imagine.

Possessives

We use the apostrophe to denote that something belongs to somebody. It would be extremely clumsy to write *the car of mother* or *the newspaper of yesterday,* so we write *mother's car* or *yesterday's newspaper.*

Where the apostrophe gets harder is when the person or thing doing the possessing ends in the letter –s. Should we write *I'm going to spend the weekend at **Mavis'** house* or *I'm going to spend the weekend at **Mavis's** house*?

It's probably best to work with the sound you want to replicate. In the case of Mavis, we would pronounce two **s's** if we spoke it aloud, so we should do the same in writing:

I'm going to spend the weekend at **Mavis's** *house?*
Charles's *car is one of the cleanest in the road.*
I have been studying **Yeats's** *poems.*

But, when the Joneses are already plural:

The window-cleaner didn't bother with the **Joneses'** *french windows this week.*

Joint Possession

When you have joint possession of something, then the apostrophe –s should come after the final item in the list:
We saw Adrian and Peter's mother.

This means that Adrian and Peter have the same mother – we saw one mother.
We went to Adrian's and Peter's christenings.

There were two separate baptisms and we went to both of them.

There is one major exception to the rule on possessives and it's the one that often causes the most confusion.
Its = belonging to it
The dog was chewing **its** *bone.*

The rule also holds for other possessive pronouns: *ours, hers, theirs, yours.*

We use the apostrophe version *it's*, when we mean *it is* or *it has*:
It's *been a long time since I went to Rome.*
It's *an ill wind that blows nobody any good.*

Missing Letters (or Numbers)

Use the apostrophe to show where there are missing letters or numbers.

182

I'm not happy with this   = *I am* not happy with this.
She's coming round tomorrow   = *She is* coming round tomorrow.
Don't think badly of me   = *Do not* think badly of me.
He hasn't finished ye   = *He has not* finished yet.
The summer of '69   = *The summer of 1969.*

Expressions of Time

Three weeks' leave... Two days' notice...

Numbers and letters

These need an apostrophe just to help the reader along:

There are two c's and two s's in the word success.
Of all the number 10's in the country, he was the best fly-half.

Common apostrophe errors:

You don't need an apostrophe if you are pluralising an abbreviation:

Does anyone know the number of MPs in the House of Commons?
My twin brother and I have identical IQs.

Similarly, it is *CDs* and *DVDs,* no matter what the sign in your local charity shop says.

The use of the apostrophe when referring to time periods is also now dropping out of fashion:

Al Capone terrorised Chicago in the 1920s and 1930s.
She wore an outfit that was straight out of the 1970s.

But, there are still tricky ones to deal with:

*She wore a **1920's** hat.*

Here 1920's is an adjective, so it has the apostrophe.

The temptation is to add an apostrophe if the noun ends in –s. No, you don't need this.

*The soldiers often had to eat in army messes (**not** mess's)*
*I've bought a Bentley to keep up with the Joneses (**not** the Jones's)*
There was a wide range of dresses in the shop (not dress's)

Nor do you need an apostrophe on the plural of nouns that end in a vowel (-a, -e, -i, -o, -u), even if that word is foreign:

Tomato	*Tomatoes*	***not** Tomato's*
Banana	*Bananas*	***not** Banana's*
Hero	*Heros*	***not** hero's*
Video	*Videos*	***not** video's*
Camera	*Cameras*	***not** camera's*

And *panini* is already plural, so it doesn't need an –s at all. Italian words ending in –*o* normally have –*i* endings in the plural. I suspect if you wanted to be ultra-pedantic during a pub meal disaster, you could say something like:

Oh dear, I have dropped a scampo on the floor.

Does the Possessive Apostrophe Matter?

I've often wondered if we couldn't just do away with the apostrophe. The Germans seem to manage pretty well without it. *Susi's book* is *Susis Buch* in German. That seems straightforward enough. I suppose there are occasions when there might be a touch of confusion, such as in the following examples with which Kingsley Amis is credited:

Those things over there are my husband's. They belong to my husband.

Those things over there are my husbands'. I've had several husbands and these are various things belonging to various husbands.

Those things over there are my husbands. I'm polygamously married to several men, none of whom is of any use. They are over there.

Brackets (Parentheses) ( )

Brackets are for containing information that is of secondary importance or explanations:

The new model (which replaces model no. 107) will be available from June.

MMU (Manchester Metropolitan University) is in the Northwest of England.

During Queen Victoria's reign (1837–1901), standards of literacy began to improve dramatically.

Additional Punctuation and Brackets

Normally, you shouldn't capitalize the first letter of anything contained in brackets, unless it's an entire sentence, or the first word needs a capital (it's a proper noun, for instance).

If you've got brackets at the end of a sentence, then using the full stop becomes slightly awkward. If the sentence is completely contained in brackets, the full stop goes inside the bracket.

There are many people who enjoy horse racing. (I am not one of them.)

If you don't have a complete sentence in the brackets, then the full stop goes outside:

We arrived back at Sidney Harbour (we'd started from there in the first place).

Square Brackets [ ]

The main use of square brackets is to explain items within

ordinary brackets: *She went to Taiwan (an island [formerly called Formosa] off the Chinese mainland).*

But it does tend to get clumsy. There are other, academic uses, but they're beyond the scope of this book and, frankly, so dull, you'll probably want to gnaw your own hand off.

- **Bullet points**

These are normally used for lists. They mean that the eye can quickly scan material. If you were to number a list, it would automatically give a kind of hierarchy to it. Bullet-points don't completely get rid of the idea that the first item on the list is more important than the last, but they do weaken that link. If you really do want item number one to be more important than item number two, and so on, then use a numbering system.

It's not hard-and-fast, but one good way of punctuating bullet-points is to punctuate normally within the bullet point (if you need commas, brackets or whatever use them), but to leave off any end punctuation. Some people do put a comma at the end of each item, then a full-stop after the last, but part of the idea of bullet-points is that they should be as uncluttered as possible. For example

Bullet points:
- *are great for lists*
- *are best kept short and uncluttered*
- *mean you can read several points quickly*
- *can be numbered (but it's probably best to avoid this)*

Emoticons and Emojis ☺

These probably don't count as punctuation as such, but I couldn't think where else to put them in this book. They are a modern method of conveying the emotion of the writer to the reader. These are mainly used in emails and other forms of electronic messaging, where the writer's tone of voice, as it were, may not come across. Emojis are even more annoying than exclamation marks. If you are going to use them, keep them for personal emails intended for the intellectually challenged, not ones that you would send in any professional capacity.

Capital Letters – CAPITALS

Not strictly punctuation either, but capital letters help us orientate ourselves when we are reading.

Sentences

The first word of a sentence starts with a capital letter:
In Britain, most of the pillar-boxes are painted red.
He had ambitions to be in the Olympic team.
We eventually solved the problem of Maria.

Names

These are normally always capitalised:
Paris   Germany   Nigel   Shropshire

Languages and adjectives relating to places

The Spanish language   Yorkshire dialect   French soldiers
But, apart from the names of languages, school subjects are no longer capitalised. They were when I was at school, so I'm always getting it wrong. So:

I am studying history, politics, film studies, Spanish and German.

If the adjective is used in a general sense, rather than

specifically about the country or people, you don't need to use capitals, but again nobody's going to shoot you if you do. In fact, the spell-checker on my word-processor has put little red lines under the following:

Hermione liked nothing better than playing russian roulette by the french windows.

Days of the Week, Months of the Year

You also need capital letters for days and months (but not the seasons):

The cruellest month is April.
I am going to meet her next Wednesday at the autumn fair.
He died on 12 September 1984.
He spent his summer weekends watching cricket.

And you thought grammar was dull…

11

Exercises — Over to you

You've managed to make it this far. It's time to let you loose and put into practice what you've learnt. The answers to most of these exercises are at the back of the book, but don't cheat and look at them first.

Exercise 1: Writing Explanations

Think through each step before beginning to write. Make a rough note of the steps needed. Put those steps into a logical order. When you have decided on the order in which to do things, work through each element as though you are a complete novice. Using simple language, explain how to do one of the following:

- Make spaghetti Bolognese
- Repair a bicycle tyre
- Tune a guitar
- Re-paint a tatty interior wall
- Find a book in a library
- Make a paper hat
- Reduce your household fuel consumption
- Give yourself a manicure and paint your nails
- Make an inexpensive soup
- Make a birthday card

- Clean out a tropical fish tank
- Wrap an unusually shaped present
- Wire a plug

Exercise 2: Confusable Words

Which is the correct word?

The dog is frightened of thunder and lightning/lightening.

I asked him a question but couldn't elicit/illicit a reply.

She found that the medicine had no affect/effect.

He was proud of the money he'd made and now felt very effluent/affluent.

I was asked to do the eulogy/elegy at her funeral.

There are two children and he is the older/oldest.

They tried to give her a bar of chocolate, but she was disinterested/uninterested.

I never do things until the last moment. I'm always prevaricating/procrastinating.

She found herself driving down a duel/dual carriageway.

The city was razed/raised to the ground.

King Henry VII proceeded/preceded King Henry VIII.

He waved/waived his right to silence.

We went to the graveyard for the interment/internment.

You shouldn't flaunt/flout the rules.

Several people caught the flu, but I was unaffected/disaffected.

The band comprised of/comprised a singer, guitarist and pianist.

Rice is the stable/staple diet of much of Asia.

I have an old pair of shoes that I keep for every day/ everyday use.

The boat foundered/floundered on the rocks.

The crowd soon disbursed/dispersed.

Exercise 3: Short and Sweet

Replace each of the following phrases with a shorter term:
- As a consequence of
- Due to the fact that
- For the purpose of
- In close proximity to
- In order to
- In the event that
- In the near future
- Initiate
- Subsequent to
- We are in a position to

Exercise 4: Dangling Participles, Misplaced Modifiers, Unclear Connections and Other Problems

Yes, we're all capable of getting things wrong, but what would you do here to clear up the mess?

After finishing his homework, the television was switched off before he decided to go to bed.

Alot of people believe in astrology.

Between you and I, there is a chance the company will go into receivership.

Closing the cupboard door, he locked it and left the building.

Driving round the corner, the lamppost hit her car.

Flying across the desert, we watched the buzzards.

He wrote a lot about music in the 1960s.

He's as hard working as I.

His eyes were fixed on the bloodstained tiles as her feet walked over them.

MP's return from their summer holidays today.

Running for the bus, the tree fell on top of him.

The flat-pack desk was assembled wrongly, not having read the instructions.

The main criteria for the job is that you need to be good with people.

The shoplifter was caught by the policeman holding the stolen items.

The woman was found guilty of stealing a coat at the magistrates' court last week.

There going to enjoy they're holiday in France when they get their.

This semi-detached house comprises of three bedrooms, a large living room, two bathrooms and a kitchen.

Visitor numbers to art galleries are down on last year. It seems less people are interested in the arts.

Walking towards home, the road works were even noisier.

You're recent pay rise probably excels you're expectations.

Exercise 5: Awkward Plurals

Not all of these are covered in the little section on awkward plurals, so you'll have to fend for yourself a little. What is the plural of:

- Crocus
- Beau
- Intelligentsia
- Hero
- Louse
- Cherub
- Passer-by
- Daughter-in-law
- Idée fixe

Exercise 6: Parts of Speech

Spot the verbs in the sentences 1–3, nouns in sentences 4–6, adjectives in 7 and 8, adverbs in 9 and 10:

1. He has been selling fruit for around ten years now.
2. The conservatory roof blew off in the gale as the wind was so strong.
3. Most readers want books that will entertain them.
4. The cat sat on the mat.
5. Norman has been selling fruit and vegetables for many years from a barrow near the station.
6. We'd like to book our tickets.
7. With a heavy heart, he began reading his long speech to the assembled crowd.
8. His elderly mother came to stay for a long-time last year.
9. When the Normans arrived, they quickly colonised most of England.
10. I often like to take a leisurely break when the sun is shining brightly.

Exercise 7: Passive and Active

Which of the following sentences are passive and which are active?
The car was hit by a run-away train.
The sky is always blue at this time of year.
He was disturbed by a stranger in a peaked cap.
The fridge has broken down again.
The Christmas lights have been put up along the high street.
There is much to be learnt from old civilisations.
I was taken by surprise.
He sat at a table by the river.
She was abducted by aliens.

Exercise 8: Punctuation

Punctuate the following, so that it makes sense for the reader.
Many people think writing is a straightforward activity all you have to do is rattle off a few words and the job is complete but it's not as simple as that before you start putting pen to paper you need to think about what it is you're trying to say you also need to think about your target readership how much jargon will they know what is their level of knowledge and education it's worth jotting down a few notes first to stir up some ideas many people like to write their first draft quickly if you're one of these that's fine but if you're not don't worry we all work in different ways and it is the end product that is important.

12

Answers and Explanations

Exercise 1: Writing Explanations

It would take up too much space here to give all the possible answers. If you've done one of these little exercises, pass it on to a friend, especially one who is not an expert on the topic you've chosen and see if they think they could carry out the task from what you've written.

Exercise 2: Confusable Words

The dog is frightened of thunder and *lightning*.

Lightening means *making more light*. *Lightning* is what you get in an electrical storm.

I asked him a question but couldn't *elicit* a reply.

Elicit means to draw out. *Illicit* means more or less the same as illegal.

She found that the medicine had no *effect*.

Effect is concerned with efficacy/effectiveness (in this context). *Affect* (again in this context) would be the verb. So we could also write *the medicine **affected** her ability to drive.*

He was proud of the money he'd made and now felt very *affluent*.

Affluent is synonymous with rich. Anyone who feels *effluent* probably has some kind of severe disorder as it is another word for sewage.

I was asked to do the *eulogy* at her funeral.

A *eulogy* is a speech of praise. An *elegy* is a kind of poem, often mourning the dead, so technically you might have an elegy at a funeral, but then you'd probably **read or recite** the *elegy*, rather than **do** the *elegy*.

There are two children and he is the *older*.

We're only comparing two people here, so we need the comparative from of the adjective *old*, and these are the ones that normally end in *-er*. If there were three children, then it would be fine to refer to the first-born as the *oldest*.

They tried to give her a bar of chocolate, but she was *uninterested*.

Uninterested means, as you'd expect, not interested in. *Disinterested*, theoretically, means not having an interest in, in the sense of being neutral. *I'm watching the football match and am not interested in who wins, therefore I am a **disinterested** spectator.* I'm now convinced that no-one knows the difference, so I hardly ever use *disinterested*.

I never do things until the last moment. I'm always *procrastinating*.

Yes, we probably know what you mean in this context, but *prevaricating* is a posh word for lying. *Procrastinating* is the posh word for putting things off.

She found herself driving down a *dual* carriageway

A *duel* involves two men, probably armed with either flintlocks or epées, facing one another in defence of a maiden's honour. *Dual* means that there are two of something. A *dual* carriageway therefore has two carriageways.

The city was *razed* to the ground.

If the city was *raised* to the ground, it must have been subterranean in the first place. Perhaps a Bond villain might press a red button and his entire city emerges from the bowels of the earth, but it's unlikely. *Razed*, here, shares the same root as your shaving blade.

King Henry VII *preceded* King Henry VIII.

Precede means to come before. *Proceed* is another way of saying *go*.

He *waived* his right to silence.

Wave is a hand gesture or a movement of water in a sea.

We went to the graveyard for the *interment.*

Interment is the posh word for a burial; *internment* that for imprisoning someone. For example, during the two World Wars, there were *internment* camps for German nationals in Britain.

You shouldn't *flout* the rules.

Rules and conventions are *flouted* when they are broken. *Flaunt* means showing off. If you're *flaunting* the rules, you've probably got them printed out on a piece of paper and are waving them around with a smug grin on your face.

Several people caught the flu, but I was *unaffected*.

Unaffected, in this context, is the opposite of affected. *Disaffected* tends to be used in contexts such as *disaffected* youths, who would be youngsters who feel as though society has little to give them.

The band *comprised* a singer, guitarist and pianist.

Comprised of is just wrong.

Rice is the *staple* diet of much of Asia.

Staple means main, in this context. *Stable* would refer to either a place to keep horses or might also mean firm or non-volatile or settled (*he's in a stable condition*).

I have an old pair of shoes that I keep for *everyday* use.

Everyday is the adjective. You would, however, write *every day I wear the same pair of old shoes*.

The boat *foundered* on the rocks.

In this context, *founder* means to run aground or hit something. *Flounder* involves flapping around. A drowning man, for instance, might *flounder*. I suspect that they often get confused because they're nearly always used for accidents at sea.

The crowd soon *dispersed*.

Dispersed means something along the lines of broken up or dissolved. *Disburse* means to pay out. You'll sometimes find it used by solicitors, who talk about *disbursements*. If you buy a house, *disbursements* might include estate agents' fees, stamp duty and the like. It refers to money that is going to be paid to the solicitor, but then paid onto someone else.

Exercise 3: Short and Sweet

As a consequence of	because
Due to the fact that	because
For the purpose of	to
In close proximity to	near
In order to	to
In the event that	if
In the near future	soon
Initiate	start
Subsequent to	following/after
We are in a position to	We can

You may have come up with perfectly good alternatives to these. Only deduct zillions of points if what you wrote was longer than the original.

Exercise 4: Dangling Participles, etc.

Of course, you may have perfectly valid alternative solutions to de-mangling, but here are my suggestions:

After finishing his homework, the television was switched off before he decided to go to bed.

Problem: We've got a bit of a mix up here with active and passive voices. Better to simplify it. Solution: *He finished his homework, switched off the television and went to bed.*

Alot of people believe in astrology.

Problem: We have a common typo here, but one that's easily put right. *A* and *lot* are two separate words. There is a word *allot*; it means something along the lines of *allocate*. Solution: *A lot of people believe in astrology.*

199

Between you and I, there is a chance the company will go into receivership.

Problem: *Between*, as a preposition, needs the object case. That 'I' is therefore wrong. Solution: *Between you and me, there is a chance the company will go into receivership.*

Closing the cupboard door, he locked it and left the building.

Problem: The implication from this sentence is that he managed to lock the cupboard and leave the building at the same time as closing the cupboard. Obviously, this is impossible. We just need to sort out the order of events. Solution: *He closed the cupboard door, locked it and left the building.*

Driving round the corner, the lamppost hit her car.

Problem: This sounds as if the lamppost is doing the driving. Solution: *As she was driving round the corner, her car hit a lamppost.*

Flying across the desert, we watched the buzzards.

Problem: We don't know who's flying? *We* or the *buzzards*? Solution: *As we were flying across the desert, we watched the buzzards.* Or: *We watched the buzzards as they flew across the desert.*

He wrote a lot about music in the 1960s.

Problem: Was he doing the actual writing in the 1960s, or is he writing about the music of that period? Solution: *In the 1960s, he wrote a lot about music.* Or: *He wrote a lot about the music of the 1960s.*

He's as hard-working as I.

Problem: You could argue that this is grammatically correct but read it out loud and you can hear that it sounds pretentious. Solution: *He's as hard-working as me.* Or: *He's as hard-working as I am.*

His eyes were fixed on the bloodstained tiles as her feet walked over them.

Problem: Is she walking on the tiles or his eyes? Solution: *His eyes were fixed on her feet as they walked across the bloodstained tiles.*

MP's return from their summer holidays today.

Problem: We've got a rogue apostrophe. Solution: *MPs return from their summer holidays today.*

Running for the bus, the tree fell on top of him.

Problem: Although it must be the 'him' who's running for the bus, this makes it sound as though it just might be the tree. It's like the lamppost in no. 5. Solution: *As he was running for the bus, the tree fell on top of him.*

The flat-pack desk was assembled wrongly, not having read the instructions.

Problem: the 'not having read the instructions' isn't attributed to anyone. It's another active/passive mix-up. Solution: *He assembled the flat-pack desk wrongly as he hadn't read the instructions.* Or, if we don't know who assembled it: *The flat-pack desk was assembled wrongly as no one had read the instructions.*

The main criteria for the job is that you need to be good with people.

Problem: *Criteria* is the plural form of the word *criterion*. Solution: *The main criterion for the job is that you need to be good with people.*

The shoplifter was caught by the policeman holding the stolen items.

Problem: It's not certain who's holding the stolen items.

Are we answering the question, 'which policeman caught the shoplifter?' – the one now holding the stolen items. Or are we telling our reader that the stolen items were in the shoplifter's hand when he was caught? Solution: *The policeman caught the shoplifter who was holding the stolen items.*

The woman was found guilty of stealing a coat at the magistrates' court last week.

Problem: This makes it sound as though she stole the coat at the magistrate's court, whereas in all likelihood she nicked it from elsewhere. Solution: *At the magistrates' court last week, the woman was found guilty of stealing a coat.*

There going to enjoy they're holiday in France when they get their.

Problem: We've mixed up there/their/they're. Yes, we know the difference, but it's so easy to do. Solution: *They're going to enjoy their holiday in France when they get there.*

This semi-detached house comprises of three bedrooms, a large living room, two bathrooms and a kitchen.

Problem: No matter what estate agents think, *comprises of* is wrong. Solution: *This semi-detached house comprises three bedrooms, a large living room, two bathrooms and a kitchen.*

Visitor numbers to art galleries are down on last year. It seems less people are interested in the arts.

Problem: You can count the number of people who go to galleries (even if only hypothetically), so you can't use 'less'. Solution: *It seems fewer people are interested in the arts.*

Walking towards home, the road works were even noisier.

Problem: It can't be the road works that are doing the walking, surely. Solution: *As he walked towards home, the road works became noisier.*

You're recent pay rise probably excels you're expectations.

Problem: There's a bit of a *your/you're* problem but give yourself bonus points if you spotted the wrong use of 'excel'. Whilst you may excel, what you actually mean is that the pay rise is greater than expected. Solution: *Your recent pay rise probably exceeds your expectations.*

Exercise 5: Awkward Plurals

Crocus – Crocuses.

Beau – Beaux (although at a pinch we'll allow beaus).

Intelligentsia – It's already plural, but being a member of it, you knew that anyway.

Hero – Heroes.

Louse – Lice.

Cherub – Cherubim (although cherubs is fine too).

Passer-by – Passers-by.

Daughter-in-law – Daughters-in-law.

Idée fixe – Idées fixes.

Alumnus – Alumni.

Exercise 6: Parts of Speech

Spot the verbs in the sentences 1-3, nouns in sentences 4-6, adjectives in 7 and 8, adverbs in 9 and 10. The answers are in the brackets.

1. He has been selling fruit for around ten years now. (*has been selling*)
2. The conservatory roof blew off in the gale as the wind was so strong. (*blew/was*)
3. Most readers want books that will entertain them. (*want/will entertain*)
4. The cat sat on the mat. (*cat/mat*)
5. Norman has been selling fruit and vegetables for many years from a barrow near the station. (*Norman/fruit/vegetables/years/barrow/station*)
6. We'd like to book our tickets. (*tickets*)
7. With a heavy heart, he began reading his long speech to the assembled crowd. (*heavy/long/assembled)*
8. His elderly mother came to stay for a long-time last year. (*elderly/long/last*)
9. When the Normans arrived, they quickly colonised most of England. (*when, quickly*)
10. I often like to take a leisurely break when the sun is shining brightly. (*often/when/brightly*)

Exercise 7: Active and Passive

The car was hit by a run-away train. (Passive)
The sky is always blue at this time of year. (Active)
He was disturbed by a stranger in a peaked cap. (Passive)
The fridge has broken down again. (Active)
The Christmas lights have been put up along the high street. (Passive)

There is much to be learnt from old civilisations. (Passive)
I was taken by surprise. (Passive)
He sat at a table by the river. (Active)
She was abducted by aliens. (Passive)

Exercise 8: Punctuation

Punctuating is not a precise art, so you may have punctuated this differently to the way I have and still be perfectly correct. This is my version:

Many people think writing is a straightforward activity. All you have to do is rattle off a few words and the job is complete, but it's not as simple as that. Before you start putting pen to paper, you need to think about what it is you're trying to say. You also need to think about your target readership. How much jargon will they know? What is their level of knowledge and education? It's worth jotting down a few notes first to help stir up some ideas. Many people like to write their first draft quickly. If you're one of these, that's fine, but if you're not, don't worry. We all work in different ways and it is the end product that is important.

Appendix 1

Useful Reading

Bad Science, Ben Goldacre (Nothing to do with writing, but if you're having to analyse data and statistics, this is a great way to start thinking about it)

Becoming a Writer, Dorothea Brande (Classic stuff and still in print after decades)

Brewer's Dictionary of Phrase and Fable

Brilliant Writing Tips for Students, Julia Copus

Collins English Dictionary (or any other top-class dictionary)

Essential English for Journalists, Editors and Writers, Harold Evans (getting long in the tooth, but great stuff)

Forgotten English, Jeffrey Kacirk (Not at all useful for helping you write, but full of fabulous words that have fallen into disuse)

How to Write Better Essays, Bryan Greetham

How to Write Dissertation & Project Reports, Kathleen McMillan & Jonathan Weyers

On Writing Well, William Zinsser

Oxford A-Z of Grammar and Punctuation, John Seely

Oxford Guide to Effective Writing and Speaking, John Seely

Oxford Guide to Plain English, Martin Cutts

Oxford Style Manual, R. M. Ritter

Planning your Essay, Janet Goodwin

Politics and the English Language, George Orwell (you can find it on-line)

Reader's Digest Reverse Dictionary (Old now, but get a second-hand copy. It's brilliant for helping find the right expression.)

Roget's Thesaurus

The Complete Plain Words, Sir Ernest Gowers.

The Elements of Style, William Strunk & E. B. White (A classic)

The Mother Tongue – English and How It Got That Way, Bill Bryson

The Mind Map Book: Unlock Your Creativity, Boost Your Memory, Change Your Life, Tony Buzan

The Penguin Dictionary of Clichés, Julia Cresswell

The Penguin Dictionary of English Grammar, R. L. Trask

The Penguin Guide to Punctuation, R. L. Trask

The Penguin Writer's Manual, Martin Manser & Stephen Curtis

Troublesome Words, Bill Bryson

Writing a Report, John Bowden

Appendix 2

How I wrote this Book

I'm hoping that the following are words of encouragement. You may be especially re-assured by the fact that my own method of writing is a shambles.

For me, planning is always the hardest part. If it's the same for you, I promise you that you are far from being alone. We scruffs look on in open-mouthed admiration at those who have neat notes and filing cabinets. We can't believe just how methodical the rest of the world seems to be. They're probably able to touch-type as well.

To console those readers who find it hard to get down to the task of writing, if I can get words onto paper, so can you. As well as being largely disorganised, I am also idle, require more caffeine than is recommended and am easily distracted.

As this is a new edition of this book, I had the luxury of being able to work from the manuscript of the original book. So, much of it is re-written from existing material. However, for the first edition, I had to start from scratch, and here's what I did, but please note that I don't have any financial interest in any of the products mentioned:

Notes

Non-fiction books such as this one are generally sold on the basis of a book proposal, which is essentially a plan of what will be contained in a book. The proposal for this book came from a mixture of notebook jottings and various teaching materials I have used over the years. I typed the essence of these up into the computer as bullet-points and every few days added (and subtracted) material as it occurred to me, often copied over from scraps of paper and little notebooks. Once I had what I thought the contents would be, I moved them round into my version of a logical shape for the book, deciding what should be dealt with in which chapter, and so forth.

It was this bare bones version of what might be in the book, fleshed out with some explanations, which I sent to my publisher. It was an outline of what the book would look like and meant that before I sat down to begin writing it 'properly', I had a list of most of the topics that I thought needed including and a potential framework for the book. Now, you may not be selling what you write, but the principle is the same – that you have some idea of where you're going with your material.

The Initial Draft

Next came the first, rough draft of the book, using the proposal as a guideline. I like to feel as though my writing has some kind of momentum. If at any point it feels as though the writing has run down a cul-de-sac, got bogged down or has lost its impetus, then I just skip to something else. For instance, the section on punctuation — not the world's most fascinating subject, but debatably more exciting than grammar — was written bit-by-bit. Dotting all over the place is fine, but it does mean that you have to sew things together at a later stage.

Avoiding Interruptions

Many people would love to work from home, so let's not make too much of a fuss about it, but there are down sides too. Years ago, when I first began writing for a living, the telephone was the great interrupter. Now it's the Internet. You have to check online constantly to see if you've had email, won that second-hand bookshelf, verify some fact, watch untalented people yodelling on YouTube or see how many close, intimate friends you now have on Facebook. Add in the easy access to music, TV, books, and even the occasional foray round the room with duster and polish, and there are far more things that you could be doing other than getting on with your writing. And the newest shiny, buy-me gadgets bring all that technology together, so that phone, email, Internet and TV are meshed almost as one. They play havoc with my fragile attention span, reducing it to that of a goldfish with a severe head injury.

To tackle this, I went back to some older-style technology. Much of the rough draft of the original version was hacked into a machine called an Alphasmart, bought on-line for the price of a couple of paperback books. The Alphasmart has a tiny screen, but a cracking keyboard and a seemingly inexhaustible battery life. Rough, first drafts can be written anywhere. As it's fiddly to edit on the machine's screen, spelling mistakes and other messes can wait until later. Once I had something that covered most of the ground, I then opened up my computer to transfer text onto my main machine.

More recently, I've gone back to sometimes writing long-hand in pencil, which means that typing up gives me a second draft without really trying. I've also swapped my Alphasmart for a Pomera (more portable, poorer keyboard) and there are newer, glossier distraction-free gadgets for writers available, such as

211

those produced by Astrohaus in America. Or you can simply disable the Wi-Fi on a laptop. Or maybe you can ignore this because you can concentrate like a proper grown-up.

If I handwrite, I use a B5 size notebook — that's halfway between A5 and A4. It's the ideal size for a project book. I write alternate lines on the right-hand page, which leaves a line for minor alterations and the left-hand page free for bigger changes or additions.

Before the work ends up in my usual word-processing program, I often use a piece of software called Scrivener. You can download a trial version to see how you get on with it. It's a mixture of text-editor-cum-corkboard (and a lot of other things). You can have every element of an enormous project open at the same time, move the chapters, or sub-chapters easily and import text from major word-processing programs. Then, when you've organised it all to your satisfaction, you compile the text in the order you want and send it through to your usual word-processing program, to tart it all up.

First Draft Completed: What Now?

Once I had smartened it all up and re-read it as a complete document, draft copies of the book went to various tame readers, 'beta-testers' as some call them, for their comments. I ignored the stupid remarks, kept the sensible ones, and threw a thank-you barbecue as the Ritz was fully booked. Then began the equally long process of shaping and re-shaping and doing my best to take out any mistakes, but there will still be some in here.

This is my way. Find your own way, but don't be surprised if your way isn't fabulously well organised. Still, I hope that this book is useful.

Good luck with your own writing projects!

Index

A

Abstract nouns, 152
Active verbs, 73
Active voice, 154
Adjectives, 69, 155, 187
Adverbs, 157
Ampersand, 166, 176
Apostrophe, 166, 181
Articles, 159
Asterisk, 166, 176
Awkward plurals, 108, 1134, 192
Awkward singulars, 108

B

Bizarre spelling, 96
Brackets, 89, 166, 185
Brainstorming, 8
Bullet points, 166, 186

C

Capital Letters, 186
Celtic, 53
Cliches, 82
Colon, 165, 167
Comma, 166, 168
Common nouns, 152
Comparatives, 110

Concrete nouns, 152
Confusable words, 118, 189
Conjunctions, 159
Countable nouns, 152

D

Dangling participles, 110
Deadlines, 24
Demonstrative pronouns, 158
Double negative, 105
Double quotation mark, 166

E

Editing, 32
Ellipsis, 166, 180
Emdash, 177
Emojis, 166, 186
Emoticons, 166, 186
Esperanto, 48
Exclamation Mark, 175

F

Finite verbs, 155
First draft, 21
Flesch Reading Ease, 65
Fonts, 47
Footnotes, 89
Full-stop, 165, 167

G
Geoffrey Chaucer, 49, 55
Grammar, 148
Gunning Fog Index, 66

H
Headings, 47
Homophones, 98
Hyphen, 166, 176

I
Intensifiers, 71
Interrogative pronouns, 158
Inverted Commas, 166, 173

J
Jargon, 61

K
Klingon, 49

L
Latinate words, 39, 54
Linear notes, 17

M
Margins, 47
Metaphors, 67
Middle English, 49
Mindmapping, 17,18

N
Non-finite verbs, 155
Noun, 151

P
Paper, 48
Paragraphs, 48, 64
Passive Sentences, 68
Passive voice, 154
Phrases, 38
Planning, 5, 13, 16
Possessive pronouns, 158
Powerful verbs, 71
Preposition, 154, 159
Pronoun, 158
Proofreading, 5, 40
Proper Nouns, 152
Psychobabble, 81
Punctuation, 94, 165

Q
Question marks, 166, 172
Quotations, 169

R
Racist writing, 85
Reflexive pronouns, 158
Repetitions, 76
Rewriting, 32

S
Semi-colon, 166, 169
Sentences, 38, 62, 64, 66
Sentence structure, 39
Sexist writing, 85
Similes, 69
Simple tenses, 72
Single quotation mark, 166

Slang, 82, 175
Spacing, 47
Split infinitive, 103
Square brackets, 166, 186
Static description, 87

T
Topic cards, 20

U
Uncountable nouns, 153

V
Verbs, 53
Vowel sounds, 179

W
Weak verbs, 40
Writer's block, 32